Glen Shee to Morven

21 Walks in Deeside

CLAN
cancer support for all

Ian Hustwick

This Guide is dedicated to Carole Munro, as without her support it would not have been written. Sadly Carole died in March 2009.

Published by Xpress Image Communications Ltd – 2009
978-0-9551642-3-1 (ISBN-13)

1st Impression April 2009 1000

FOREWORD

This Guide was written with the intention of giving routes for walks in Upper Deeside as well as providing information about Geological and Archaeological features and Birds and Plants which could be seen on these walks. I realised that when surveying the routes, my knowledge of these subjects was limited, and I assumed that other walkers would also wish to widen their knowledge of the countryside.

To obtain this information, it was necessary to approach a wide range of people who knew the area such as the Aberdeenshire Ranger Service and Scottish Natural Heritage. They in turn advised me to approach others who were very well-qualified to provide information on Geology, Archaeology and Plants and who answered all my questions and provided information on various sources. Obtaining this knowledge and visiting the various sites proved to be very enjoyable – almost as much as surveying the walks. Without the help of a wide range of very pleasant and interesting people, this Guide could not have been written.

There are many more interesting features and plant sites to be found in this area and I hope that the information provided in this Guide will encourage walkers to seek them out.

All the proceeds from the sale of this Guide, are used to support Cancer Link Aberdeen and North (CLAN), a charity serving people directly and indirectly affected by a diagnosis of cancer, throughout North East Scotland, Orkney and Shetland.

Ian Hustwick
Aberdeen 2009

ACKNOWLEDGEMENTS

This Guide would not have been published without the positive support of Susan Crighton, CLAN's Fund Raising Manager and Debra Coe, Fund Raising Assistant, and I am very grateful for their support. The efforts of CLAN Volunteer, Pat Mundie, who kindly typed the booklet with patience and skill in deciphering my hand script, was much appreciated.

I am also grateful to the following people and organisations without whose help this Guide would not have been published.

Geology: Rachel Wignall of Scottish Natural Heritage wrote the appendix dealing with the Formation of the Landscape and who is far better qualified than myself in the writing on this particular subject. Mrs Jane Angus, Ballater, for providing information on the structure of the rocks in each walk and on many other items.

Plants: Mrs C. Fallowfied, Braemar; Professor Gimmingham, Aberdeen; Andrea Britton, Macaulay Institute, Aberdeen; Heather McHaffie and David Long, Royal Botanic Gardens, Edinburgh; Catriona Reid, Mike Smedley and James Dey, Scottish Natural Heritage, Aberdeen.

Archaeology: Mrs Greig, Archaeology Department, Aberdeenshire Council; Miriam McDonald, Royal Commission for Ancient and Historical Monuments of Scotland, Edinburgh, Dr Hutcheon, Aberdeen, on living conditions in the 17th/18th Centuries; Mrs Jane Angus, Ballater, for information on Lime Kilns; and Bob Powell, Highland Folk Museum, Newtonmore for information on Shielings.

Birds: Drs James R. Graham and I.S. Frances, Royal Society for the Protection of Birds, Aberdeen.

Photographs: These were supplied by Scottish Natural Heritage, Aberdeen, and Scottish Natural Heritage, Battleby, Perth. The picture on the front cover has been taken from my own records. Pictures of the Lichens were provided by Andrea Britton, Macaulay Research Institute, Aberdeen. Pictures of Club Mosses and Mosses were provided by Helen McHaffie and David Long respectively, both of Royal Botanic Garden, Edinburgh. I am grateful to the Royal Commission of Ancient and

Historical Monuments of Scotland for permission to reproduce the map of Western Aberdeenshire, shown on the back cover of the Guide.

I am grateful to Mr and Mrs Malcolm Smith for surveying the route of Carn an Tuirc and providing a detailed report on the area and also in checking the manuscript, as did Ian Bryce who also made very relevant comments. Last but not least, Mike Daw for final editing and checking before publication of the Guide.

Information on certain areas of Upper Deeside was given by Mrs Helen Rowe, Countryside Ranger for South Mar, Aberdeenshire Council; Eric Baird, Ranger, Glen Tanar Estate; Fiona Smith, Glen Muick Visitor Centre; Glyn Jones, Ranger, Balmoral Estate; and Peter Fraser, Gamekeeper, Glen Callater.

Last but not least, with great thanks to John Morrison, Shona McIntosh and their colleagues at Xpress Image Communications for all their help and support in getting this book to the stage it is at today, a comprehensive published guide for walkers. It took great expertise and patience to turn my idea into a reality and for that I am extremely grateful.

GUIDANCE NOTES

As the scale given in the Landranger Series does not provide sufficient detailed Maps we have taken maps from the Explorer Series for certain walks.

The estimated times to complete a walk and the distance to be covered are given so that walkers can use their own judgement to ascertain how long each walk could take and for this reason the walks have not been graded. The times given for each walk does not include times for coffee and lunch breaks. All walks are on good tracks on paths, with the exception of two – Greystone to Deecastle and Morven Lodge where there are no paths (for a short distance). The height given for the walk has been measured by deducting the height at the car park from the highest point on the walk.

While the majority of the walks are below 700 m, the first five walks and Walks 5 and 21 are Munros and Corbetts where conditions can, and do, change during the day. It is essential that these walks are not undertaken unless with a companion, a compass and map are carried, and a check is made of the weather forecast. At 900 m it can be very cold. Severe variations of the weather are unlikely on the other walks. Nevertheless an Ordnance Survey map and a compass should be carried, together with adequate wind and waterproof clothing. Accidents can, and do, happen so as far as possible climb with a companion. A mobile phone is always necessary although reception in certain areas can be poor. It is also sensible to leave details of your planned route with estimated time of return, with a friend or the person you are staying with. Always carry a supply of water (never less than one litre), adequate food, dried fruit and energy bars.

Please observe the Scottish Outdoor Access Code and its three principles, given below.

Respect the interests of other people: Be considerate, respect privacy and livelihoods, and the needs of those enjoying the outdoors.

Care for the Environment: Look after the places you visit and enjoy them. Care for wildlife and historic sites.

Take responsibility for your own actions.

Also, the **Walking Safety Code:**

1. Walk in single file on the right hand side of the road.
2. Face oncoming traffic.
3. Warn others of approaching traffic.

The Canadian Rule also applies to Scotland – **TAKE ONLY PHOTOGRAPHS LEAVE ONLY FOOTPRINTS**.

RECOMMENDED READING

Deserted Farms and Shielings in the Braemar Area, John Smith, Proc. of Soc. Antiq. Vol 116, (1986).

The Place Names of Upper Deeside, Watson and Allan, Aberdeen University Press.

Mar Lodge Estate, Royal Commission on the Ancient and Historical Monuments of Scotland.

The Lime Kilns of Upper Donside, Archeological Department, Aberdeenshire Council, (2004).

Introducing Geology, Graham Park, Dundee Academies Press, (2006).

Landscape of Mountain and Flood, McKirdy, Gordon and Croft, SNH (1997).

Cairngorms: A Landscape Fashioned by Geology, SNH (2006).

Hostile Habitats, Edited by Kempe and Wrightham, Scottish Mountaineering Trust (2006).

Grasses, Ferns, Mosses and Lichens, Pan Books (2009).

Lichens, Purvis, Natural History Museum (2000).

Montane Heathland Lichen, Britton, Macaulay Institute, Aberdeen (2008).

Scottish Wild Plants, Lusby and Wright, Royal Botanic Gardens, Edinburgh, Mercat Press Ltd, (2001).

Flora Celtica, Maliken and Bridgewater, Royal Botanic Gardens, Edinburgh, (2006).

The Scots Herbal, Darwin, Mercat Press Ltd, (2008).

Scottish Wild Flowers, Michael Scott, Collins, (2000).

Scottish Birds, Valerie Thom, Harper Collins, (2006).

LIST OF WALKS

+ Difference between the height at the car park and that of the highest point on the walk

APPENDICES

* Information on birds seen on each walk is contained in the above mentioned Appendix 5.

1. GLAS MAOL, (THE GREEN HILL) AND CREAG LEACACH (ROCKY HILL) LANDRANGER MAP 43

These hills, both Munros, are included for two reasons. Their summits are close to the starting point and they give good views of Glen Shee and Glen Clunie and the climb to Glen Maol, although steep, can be done in two stages. The path in the second stage is well graded so there are plenty of opportunities to admire the views. This is a walk which should only be done if the visibility is good in order to enjoy the scenery. Times are given for each hill for walkers who wish only to do Glas Maol. (Map, Compass and Boots are essential).

Access: The starting point for this walk is the car park at Glenshee Ski Centre where there are toilet facilities.

Glas Maol Route: At the south side of the car park, take a stony track which goes steeply uphill and then descends to a flat area at the foot of Meall Odhar. A well graded path goes up this hill to a flat area before a short climb up to moorland where the cairn, marking the summit of Glas Maol, will be seen.

9 km 4½ hrs net ht 403 m

Creag Leacach Route: The summit of Creag Leacach is at the end of the ridge connecting it to Glas Maol. The path is downhill and follows a dyke which leads to the summit. There is wire lying along this route, which is otherwise free of hazards. The climb to the summit involves an easy scramble up a boulder-clad slope.

15 km 6½ hrs net ht 403 m

Geology: The plateau to the east of Meall Odhar and Glen Maol is mainly grass due to the underlying strata being composed of calcareous rock.

Flowers: Heather, Bell Heather, Cloudberry, Cranberry (Cowberry), Trailing Azalea, Mountain Everlasting, Tormentil, Dwarf Willow, Starry Saxifrage, Dwarf Cudweed, Alpine Lady's Mantle, Crowberry, Yellow Mountain Saxifrage.

Club Mosses: Fir 1,300m, Alpine 1,200m, Stags Horn 840m, Interrupted 1,000m, maximum height of growth.

Mosses: Sphagnums Capillifolium and Palustre, Philonotis Fontana, Polytrichum Commune.

Lichens: Ochrolechia Frigida, Ochrolechia Tartarea, Thamnolia Vermicularis, Cladonia Rangiferina (Reindeer Moss), Flavocetraria Nivalis.

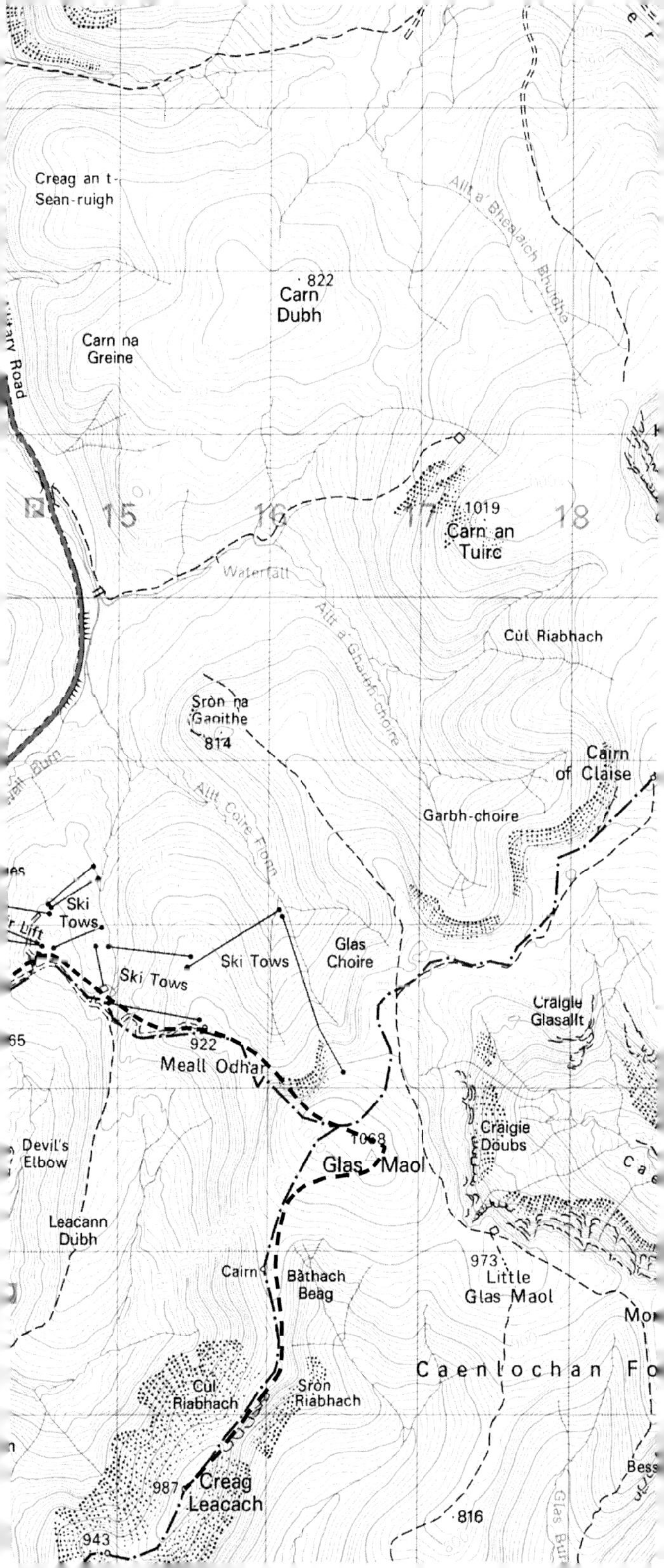

Creag an t-
Sean-ruigh
822
Carn
Dubh
Carn na
Greine
Allt a' Bhealaich Bhuidhe
15
16
17
18
1019
Carn an
Tuirc
Waterfall
Allt a' Gharbh-choire
Cùl Riabhach
Sròn na
Gaoithe
814
Cairn
of Claise
Allt Coire Fionn
Garbh-choire
Ski
Tows
Ski Tows
Ski Tows
Glas
Choire
Craigie
Glasallt
922
Meall Odhar
1068
Glas Maol
Craigie
Doubs
Devil's
Elbow
Leacann
Dubh
Cairn
Bàthach
Beag
973
Little
Glas Maol
Caenlochan
Cùl
Riabhach
Sròn
Riabhach
987
Creag
Leacach
943
816

2. GLAS MAOL, CREAG LEACACH AND SPITTAL OF GLENSHEE LANDRANGER MAP 43

The walk follows the same route as Walk 1 and then continues down over the grass-covered hills to the Spittal. A pleasant downhill walk with good views over the Glenshee Hills which should only be undertaken in good weather. There is no path for the first part of the walk and it is necessary to go towards Sron na Fionnach to join the path to the Spittal which is easy to do when there is good visibility. As it is a very long walk up Glen Shee this walk requires two cars.

14 km 6 hrs net ht 403 m

Route: There is only one track on this walk which starts at the eastern end of the route on the slope of Sron Na Fionnach (Grid Ref 123 7/6). After leaving Creag Leacach go in the direction of Carn Ait and Carn Aig Mhala. Although there are paths in places, it is a case of keeping to the high ground and going in the direction of Sron na Fionnach and the track on the eastern slope. This track leads down to the Spittal of Glenshee.

Geology: The rock underlying Glas Maol is schist which is easily eroded and provides the nutrients for plants at its summit. A similar strata underlies Creag Leacach. The strata which underlies the hill in Glen Shee is calcareous which is the reason for the hills being covered in grass.

Flowers: Heather, Bell Heather, Cloudberry, Cranberry (Cowberry), Trailing Azalea, Mountain Everlasting, Tormentil, Dwarf Willow, Starry Saxifrage, Dwarf Cudweed, Alpine Lady's Mantle, Crowberry, Yellow Mountain Saxifrage.

Club Mosses: Fir 1,300m, Alpine 1,200m, Stags Horn 840m, Interrupted 1,000m, maximum height of growth.

Mosses: Sphagnums Capillifolium and Palustre, Philonotis Fontana, Polytrichum Commune.

Lichens: Ochrolechia Frigida, Ochrolechia Tartarea, Thamnolia Vermicularis, Cladonia Rangiferina (Reindeer Moss), Flavocetraria Nivalis.

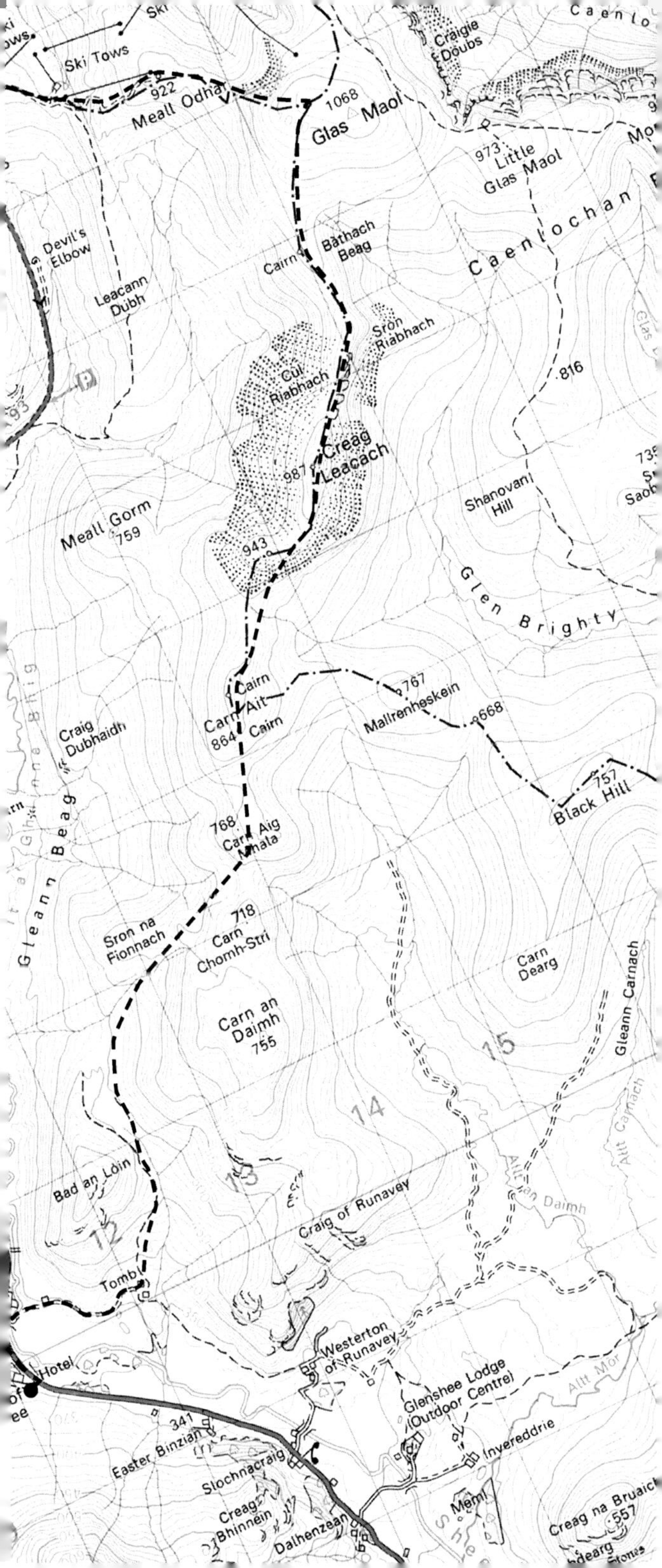

Ski Tows
922
Meall Odhar
1068
Glas Maol
Craigie Doubs
973
Little Glas Maol
Caenlochan
Devil's Elbow
Leacann Dubh
Cairn
Bàthach Beag
Sron Riabhach
Cul Riabhach
816
Creag Leacach
987
943
Shanovan Hill
Meall Gorm
759
Glen Brighty
Cairn
Carn Ait
864
Cairn
767
Mallrenheskein
668
Craig Dubhaidh
Black Hill
757
Gleann Beag
768
Carn Aig Mhala
718
Sron na Fionnach
Carn Chomh-Stri
Carn an Daimh
755
Carn Dearg
Gleann Carnach
15
14
13
12
Bad an Loin
Craig of Runavey
Allt an Daimh
Allt Carnach
Tomb
Hotel
Westerton of Runavey
Glenshee Lodge (Outdoor Centre)
Allt Mor
341
Easter Binzian
Slochnacraig
Inverreddrie
Creag Bhinnein
Dalhenzean
Creag na Bruaich
557

3. CARN AN TUIRC (HILL OF THE BOAR) AND CORRIE KANDER (CEANNDAIR, CORRIE OF THE HEADWATER) LANDRANGER MAP 43

Carn an Tuirc forms the rim of a plateau together with Cairn of Claise and Glas Maol. The plateau is of interest due to the range of birds that can be seen as well as providing pleasant walking on the tracks that traverse it. The paths to the summit and from the Corrie to Cairn of Claise are not always easy to follow and inexperienced walkers should if possible avoid this walk unless the weather is good. Corrie Kander gives an opportunity to look at a corrie which is noted for being a site for alpine flowers and rare minerals. (Map, Compass and Boots are essential).

12 km 4½ hrs net ht 510 m

Access: There are two car parks on the A93, one of which is marked on the map and another which is higher up where there is a gap in the crash barrier (Grid Ref 148 800). The walk can start at either of these car parks as there is a track on the other side of the road from the lower car park which leads to the bridge. No charge. Toilet facilities at Glenshee car park.

Route: Starting at the upper car park, cross the old bridge and follow a muddy path that goes up beside the burn and ascends towards the north side of the summit and from there climb to the summit, (2 hrs). Descend on the east face and walk to the Corrie, (30 mins). The return is made by walking over a broad ridge on a track which disappears so follow a line of posts which leads to Cairn of Claise (30 mins). Descend towards the rim of the Garbh Choire and follow the old Monega Road. This goes along the north face of Sron na Gaoithe and descends to meet the burn which leads to the car park.

Archaeology: The present A93 follows in part the line of the road built by the Government after the 1745 uprising, supplying garrisons in Braemar, Corgarff and Fort George. The old bridge was built in 1748 and the old road continues down to the lower car park. The garrison at Braemar was there for two reasons – initially to hunt for Jacobites and latterly to protect the passage of cattle. There was a hospice at Sean Spittal which, in medieval times, gave shelter to people crossing over the Monega Mounth, the highest mounth in Scotland. There are two shieling areas near to the path at the base of the hill. The upper area contains more sites, some of which are large, an indication perhaps of farming activities in addition to just summer grazing.

Geology: The summit of Carn an Tuirc is composed of quartzite and below it there are bands of dolomite and schist. It is these rocks which provide the nutrients for the grasses for the shieling sites at 630 m and lower down. Corrie Kander is composed of lime-rich schists which provide the nutrients for the many plants in the corrie. The corrie contains deposits of barium, sulphur, zinc, lead and silver.

For walkers who have done this hill and have other interests, there are areas worth taking time to visit, such as the Upper Shieling area, to ascertain the different building sites, long houses, corn kilns and pens. Walking up to the waterfall and continuing up Allt a' Gharbh Choire or Allt a Cul Riabhach one can examine the rock formation and in the upper reaches, the location of mountain flowers where there are calcareous rocks.

Flowers: Heather, Bell Heather, Cloudberry, Cranberry (Cowberry), Trailing Azalea, Mountain Everlasting, Tormentil, Dwarf Willow, Starry Saxifrage, Dwarf Cudweed, Alpine Lady's Mantle, Crowberry, Yellow Mountain Saxifrage.

Club Mosses: Fir 1,300m, Alpine 1,200m, Stags Horn 840m, Interrupted 1,000m, maximum height of growth.

Mosses: Sphagnums Capillifolium and Palustre, Philonotis Fontana, Polytrichum Commune.

Lichens: Ochrolechia Frigida, Ochrolechia Tartarea, Thamnolia Vermicularis, Cladonia Rangiferina (Reindeer Moss), Flavocetraria Nivalis.

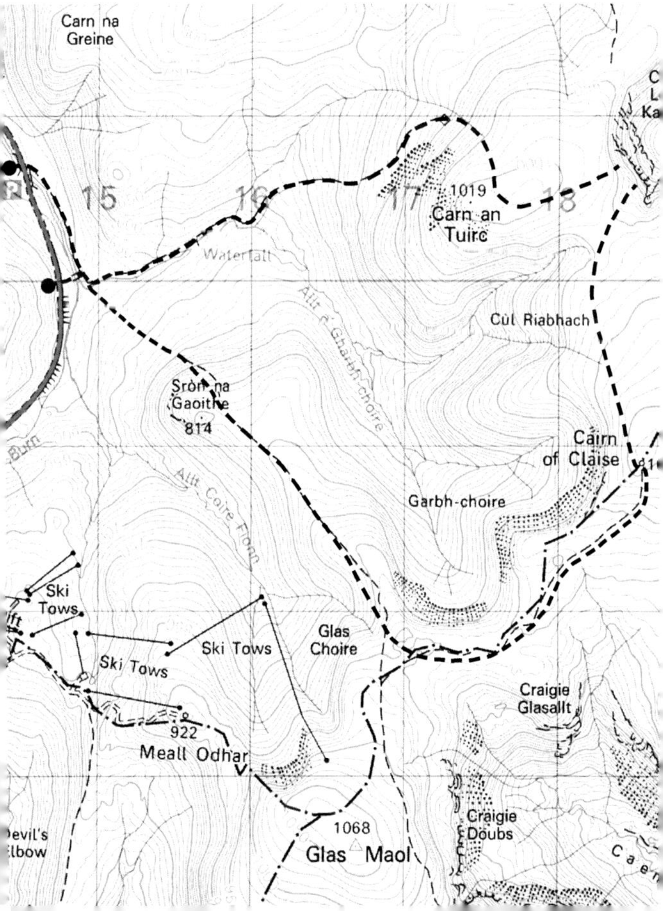

4. CAIRNWELL, CARN A' GHEOIDH (HILL OF THE GOOSE), AND CARN AOSDA LANDRANGER MAP 42

These three Munros are situated to the west of the Glenshee Ski Centre. They are situated on the rim of a large flat area and connected by good paths and do not involve much climbing. The circuit of the three tops provide a good panoramic view of surrounding hills. This is a walk which should only be done if the visibility is good in order to enjoy the scenery. (Map, Compass and Boots are essential).

10 km 4 hrs net ht 310 m

Access: The starting point for this walk is the car park at Glenshee Ski Centre where there are toilet facilities (Grid Ref 139 780).

Route: If the cable car is not working, walk round the northern shoulder of the Cairnwell and climb up the ridge at its lowest point to the path which runs from the Cairnwell to Carn Aosda. Turn left and climb the Cairnwell, descend to the path which goes to Carn a' Gheoidh. Return by the same route and join the path leading to Carn Aosda. The track from that hill goes directly to the car park.

Geology: The area covered by these three hills is composed of granite with the exception of Loch Vrotachan which is situated in dolomitic limestone.

Flowers: The area to the west of the Cairnwell has crumbly limestone which supports plants such as Thyme, Mountain Everlasting, Field Gentian, Alpine Lady's Mantle, Hairbell, Purple and Yellow Saxifrage, Alpine Meadow Rue, Northern Bedstraw, Alpine Cinquefoil, Speedwell, Mouse Ear. The site for Alpine Milkwort is on either side of the path from the Cairnwell and Carn a' Gheoidh.

Club Mosses: Fir 1,300m, Alpine 1,200m, Stags Horn 840m, Interrupted 1,000m, maximum height of growth.

Mosses: Sphagnums Capillifolium and Palustre, Philonotis Fontana, Polytrichum Commune.

Lichens: Ochrolechia Frigida, Ochrolechia Tartarea, Thamnolia Vermicularis, Cladonia Rangiferina (Reindeer Moss), Flavocetraria Nivalis.

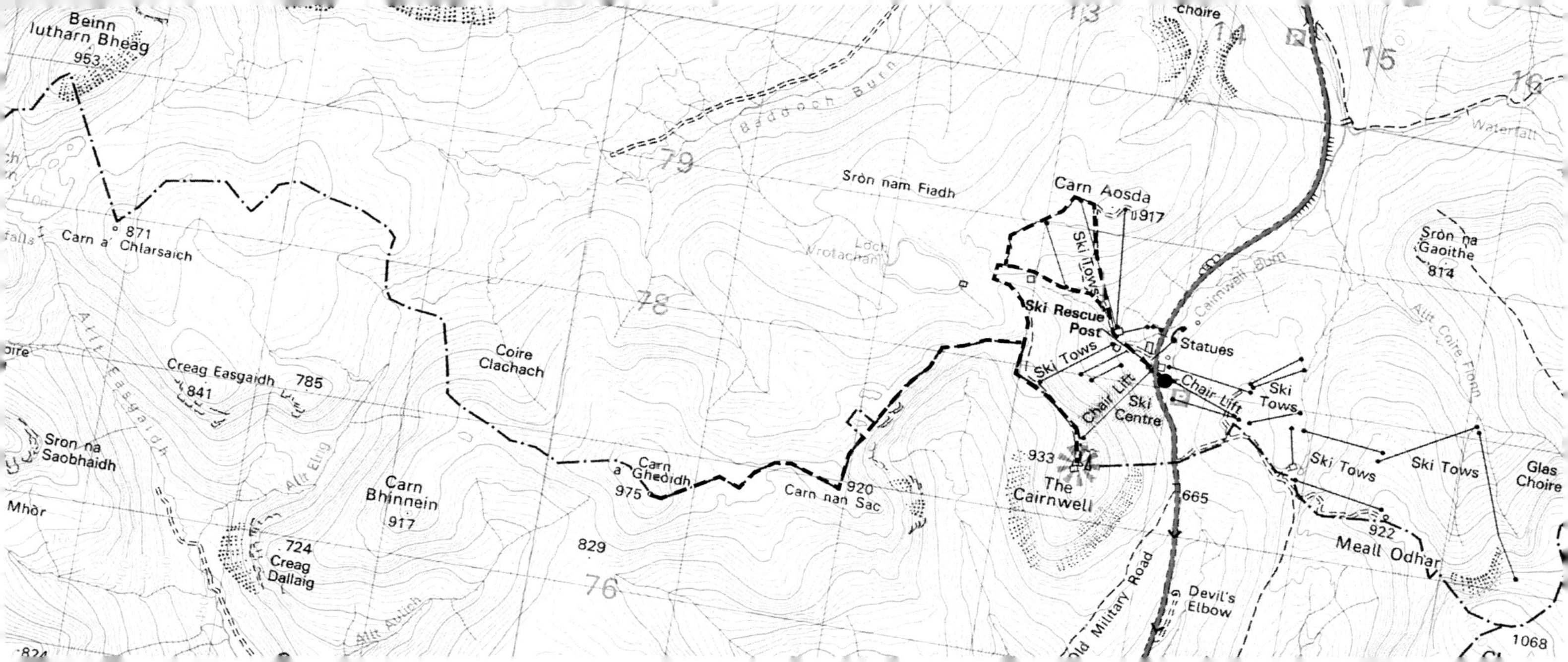
Beinn Iutharn Bheag
953
871
Carn a' Chlarsaich
Creag Easgaidh
841
785
Allt Easgaidh
Sron na Saobhaidh
Mhòr
Carn Bhinnein
917
724
Creag Dallaig
829
76
Coire Clachach
78
79
Baddoch Burn
Carn a' Gheoidh
975
920
Carn nan Sac
Sròn nam Fiadh
Loch Vrotachan
Carn Aosda
917
Ski Tows
Ski Rescue Post
Ski Tows
Chair Lift
Ski Centre
933
The Cairnwell
665
Statues
Cairnwell Burn
Chair Lift
Ski Tows
Ski Tows
Ski Tows
Glas Choire
922
Meall Odhar
Devil's Elbow
Old Military Road
1068
Sròn na Gaoithe
814
Allt Coire Fionn
Waterfall
13
14
15
16

5. CREAG NAN GABHAR (ROCKY HILL OF THE GOATS) LANDRANGER MAP 43

A good walk along a broad ridge to a summit which gives views of Glen Callater and Glen Shee. The top provides a good view of Loch Callater and the hills to the south as well as the Glen Shee hills. According to Peter Fraser, keeper of Glen Callater, there are no goats as they died through natural causes in the 1950s. (Map, Compass and Boots are essential if going down to the lodge) .

12 km 4½ hrs net ht 430 m

Access: Park at the area just off the A93 at the entrance to Glen Callater which is the starting point for the walk (Grid Ref 156 883). No charge for parking and no toilet facilities.

Route: The track up to the hill branches off to the left 20 minutes after leaving the car park and goes up past the shoulder of Sron Dubh (Black Nose), (45 mins). The track turns south along the ridge to Sron nan Gabhar where it becomes a path (10 mins). The path soon disappears which presents no difficulty as the surface is dry and easy to traverse to the summit (15 mins). The return journey may be made by using the same route or by descending to the track which goes through the Bealach Buidhe. At the fork in Glen Callater take the path leading to the lodge. There is a shieling site at the end of the path and another a short distance further down the glen.

Geology: This hill is mainly composed of quartzite. The area between the summit and Callater Lodge is composed of dolomitic limestone and schist and it is these rocks which provide the nutrients for the two shielings situated beside the lodge and a short distance down from the loch.

Flowers: Heather, Cranberry (Cowberry), Bell Heather, Blaeberry, Hare's Tail Cotton Grass, Cloudberry, Sundew, Bog Asphodel, Butterwort, Cross-leaved Heath, Thyme.

Club Mosses: Fir 1,300m, Alpine 1,200m, Stags Horn 840m, Interrupted 1,000m, maximum height of growth.

Mosses: Sphagnums Capillifolium and Palustre, Philonotis Fontana, Polytrichum Commune.

Lichens: Ochrolechia Frigida, Ochrolechia Tartarea, Thamnolia Vermicularis, Cladonia Rangiferina (Reindeer Moss), Flavocetraria Nivalis.

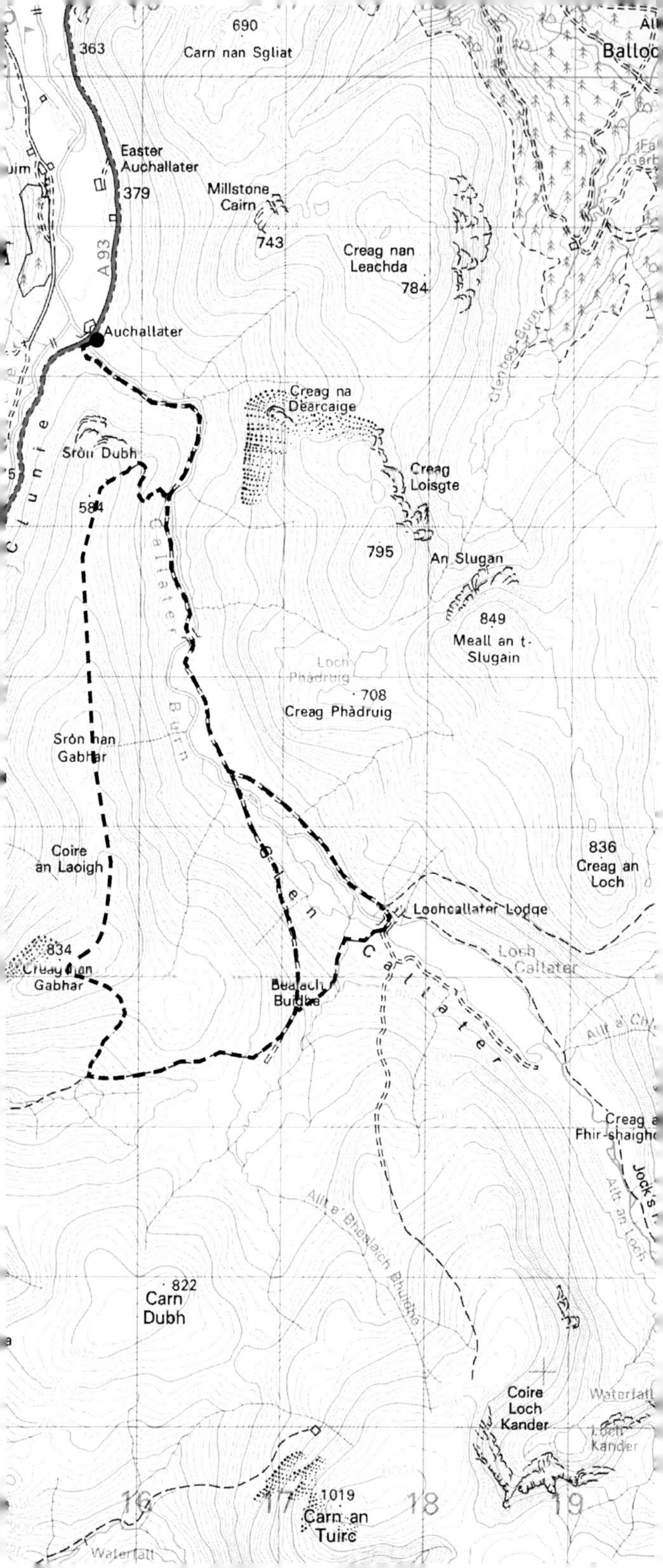

690
Carn nan Sgliat
363
Easter
Auchallater
379
Millstone
Cairn
743
A93
Creag nan
Leachda
784
Auchallater
Glenbeg Burn
Creag na
Dearcaige
Sròn Dubh
584
Creag
Loisgte
795
An Slugan
849
Meall an t-
Slugain
Loch
Phàdruig
708
Creag Phàdruig
Callater Burn
Clunie
Sròn nan
Gabhar
836
Creag an
Loch
Coire
an Laoigh
Glen Callater
Lochcallater Lodge
Loch
Callater
834
Creag nan
Gabhar
Bealach
Buidhe
Creag a
Fhir-shaighde
Allt a' Bhealaich Bhuidhe
Jock's
Allt an Loch
822
Carn
Dubh
Coire
Loch
Kander
Waterfall
Loch
Kander
16
17
1019
Carn an
Tuirc
18
19
Waterfall

6. GLEN CONNIE
LANDRANGER MAP 43

This is a walk up an old road which served as an access for peat cutting and the shielings which occupied many sites in the glen. It is a pleasant glen for two reasons, to explore two small glens and their shieling sites, and to go to the head of the glen to obtain good views of Beinn a' Ghlo and the western Cairngorms. For more energetic walkers who wish to obtain a panoramic view of the Cairngorms they should continue up to the summit of Carn Liath and then back along the ridge to Inverey. Details of the walk are given in my book "Durris to Luibeg".

Shieling Sites 10 km 3½ hrs net ht 150 m

Top of Glen 14 km 4 hrs net ht 400 m

Access: This walk starts at the car park at Inverey, 7 km from Braemar – no charge for parking and no toilet facilities (Grid Ref 089 891).

Route: Follow the tarred road to the bridge and turn left past the house and then turn right up the hill into Glen Connie to a point where a small glen will be seen on the left (45 mins). There is a track (Grid Ref 074 871) going down on the left and which continues up the glen where it stops beside the site of three dwellings beside the burn (25 mins). The RCAHMS Survey of Mar Estate gives a map of the area showing some 20 sites. Many of these sites are covered by heather as are some original grazing areas. The Allt Cristie Mor which flows down this glen is gaelic for the burn of the firewood. The shieling folk must have burnt all the timber for there are now no trees in the glen.

There is another small glen further up Glen Connie through which flows the Allt Cristie Beag (the swift one), 25 mins. There is a path (Grid Ref 056 869), partially hidden by the heather, will be seen which goes down to this area where there are several remains of dwellings, all connected by paths. These sites are quite close to the path up the glen. A large grazing area will be seen further up Glen Connie where, according to the RCAHMS map, there are more shieling sites. A walk to look at shielings may not be to everybody's taste so continue up to the top of the glen where Beinn Y Ghloe and the western Cairngorms can be seen on a clear day (Grid Ref 034 865). *(See Appendix 2 for more information on shielings).*

Geology: In the upper slopes of both Allt Cristie Mor and Allt Cristie Beag there are deposits of calcareous rock which contain sufficient nutrients for the grass which grows in these glens.

Flowers: Heather, Bell Heather, Cranberry (Cowberry), Cloudberry, Bog Asphodel, Bird's Foot Trefoil, Hare's Tail Cotton Grass, Heath Spotted Orchid, Butterwort, Sundew, Thyme.

Club Mosses: Fir 1,300m, Alpine 1,200m, Stags Horn 840m, Interrupted 1,000m, maximum height of growth.

Mosses: Sphagnums Capillifolium and Palustre, Philonotis Fontana, Polytrichum Commune.

Lichens: Ochrolechia Frigida, Ochrolechia Tartarea, Thamnolia Vermicularis, Cladonia Rangiferina (Reindeer Moss), Flavocetraria Nivalis.

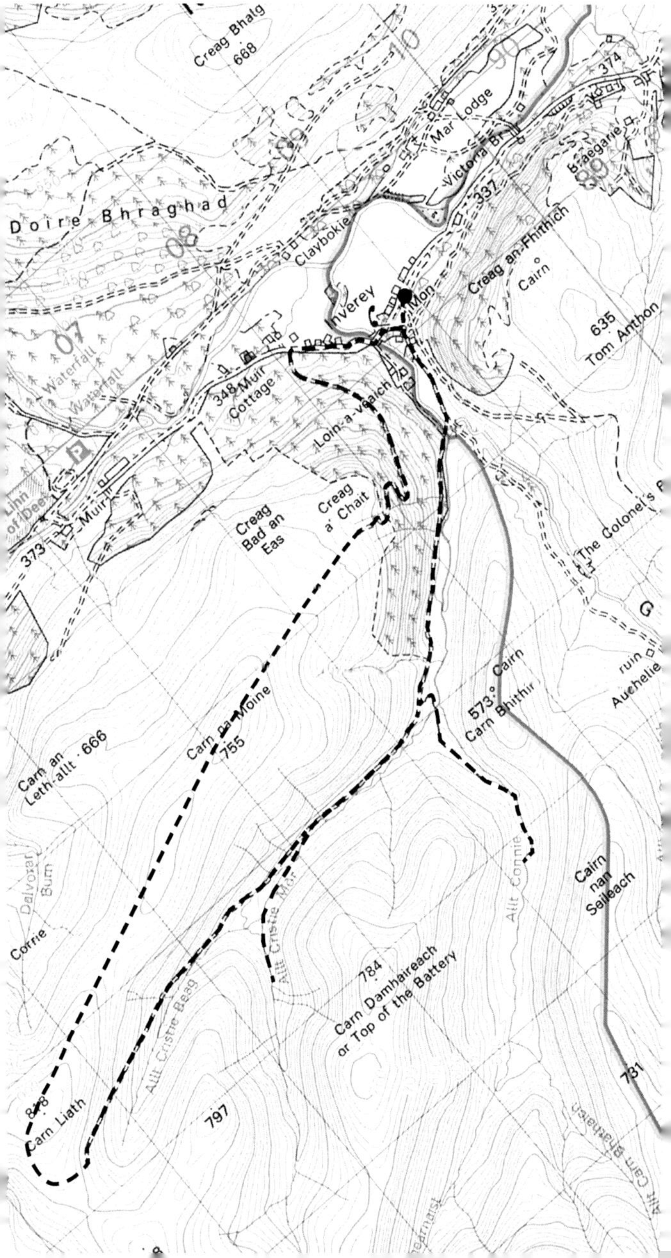

7. INVEREY, CARN MOR (BIG HILL), TOM ANTHON AND CORRIEMULZIE (CORRIE OF THE MILL) LANDRANGER MAP 42

Carn Mor, although not well known, is included because it gives good views of the Cairngorms, Carn Liath and Glen Ey. Glen Ey was well populated from the 17th to the 19th Century as it was sheltered and fertile.

14 km 3 hrs net ht 210 m

Access: The starting point is the car park at Inverey, 7 km from Braemar. No parking fee (Grid Ref 089 891). No charge or toilet facilities.

Route: The track goes past the houses and turns left up the hill going past a col, (45 mins) and then continues round the shoulder of Carn Mor to the summit which is not well defined. There is limited shelter at the end of the path, (1 hr 20 mins).

The return journey can be made by taking the same route or by going through the col and down to Corriemulzie. The path through the col is of variable quality as it disappears at intervals so keep to the left side of the burn. The path lower down is very much easier to follow. Where the burn joins the Corriemulzie burn there are the remains of an old lime kiln. The path then goes up through a birch wood where it meets a good track which goes to the mill at Corriemulzie. From there, go along the road for a short distance, cross the dyke and head for a gate in the woods which is the entrance to a track to the car park, (30 mins).

Geology: The col between Tom Anthon and Carn Mor is part of a fault line which runs from Glen Gairn to Glen Tilt. This col may have been a meltwater channel. Tom Anthon's base is composed of dolomitic limestone which extends down the col and around it to the north side of the hill. This strata of limestone was quarried to provide stone for the kiln.

Archaeology: There are three grassed areas in Glen Ey which are underlain by calcareous rock. The largest is on the shoulder of Carn Bhithir which is just opposite Carn Mor on the other side of the Ey, where there are several shieling sites as well as the remains of a site which was occupied from the 12th to the 19th centuries. Halfway up the glen there is another area on the east bank of the Ey. The area with the largest number of sites starts before the Altanour Lodge and continues beyond it. This area contains sites of larger buildings and corn kilns indicating a permanent settlement.

Flowers: Cross-leaved Heath, Yellow Saxifrage, Common Dog Violet, Alpine Cinquefoil, Golden Saxifrage, Coltsfoot, Common Rockrose, Mountain Everlasting, Germander Speedwell, Eyebright, Thyme, Butterwort, Heath Spotted Orchid, Heather, Cranberry (Cowberry), Alpine Bistort, Hare's Tail Cotton Grass, Wood Anemone.

Club Mosses: Fir 1,300m, Alpine 1,200m, Stags Horn 840m, Interrupted 1,000m, maximum height of growth.

Mosses: Sphagnums Capillifolium and Palustre, Philonotis Fontana, Polytrichum Commune.

Lichens: Ochrolechia Frigida, Ochrolechia Tartarea, Thamnolia Vermicularis, Cladonia Rangiferina (Reindeer Moss), Flavocetraria Nivalis.

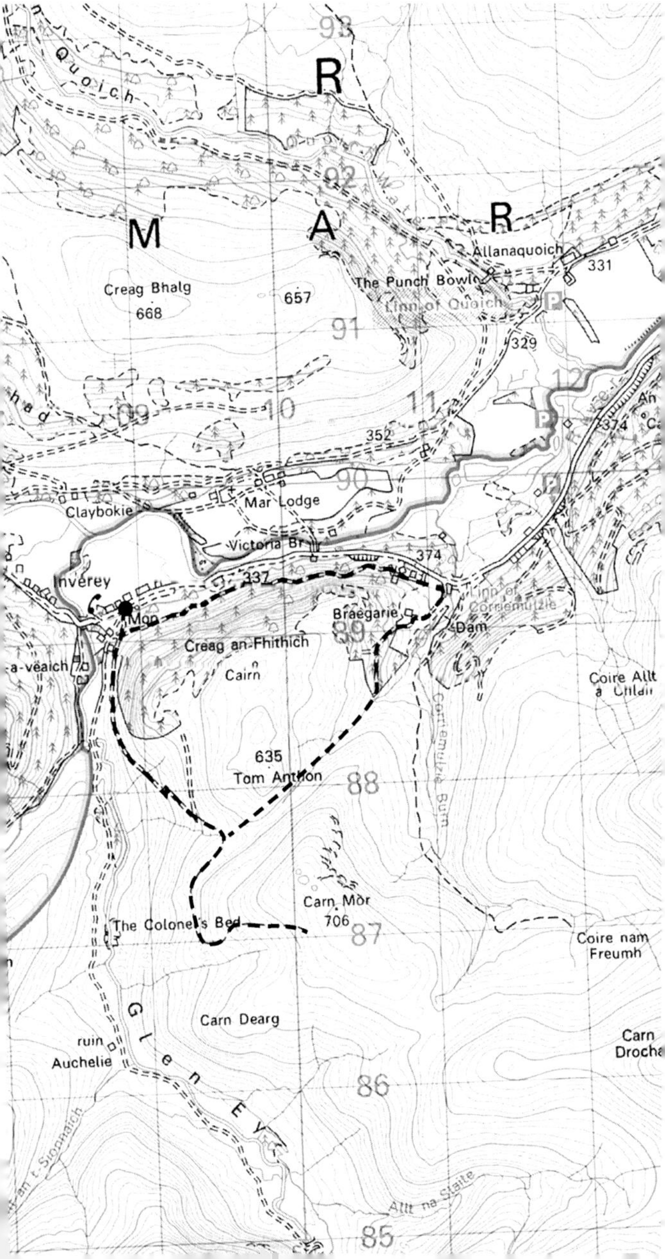

8. LOCH PHADRUIG (PATRICK'S LOCH) LANDRANGER MAP 42

This is a small loch on the east side of Loch Callater which is easily accessible from the road up Glen Callater. The hills surrounding the loch are good viewpoints for Loch Callater. The path through the small bealach to the north east of the loch looks down on Ballochbuie Forest. There are interesting plants which grow at the fringe of the loch. (Boots essential).

7 km 2½ hrs net ht 310 m

Access: Park at an area just off the A93 at the entrance to Glen Callater which is the starting point for the walk (Grid Ref 158 883).

Route: Follow the track up the glen as far as the bridge, 3 km, which is the starting point for the path to the loch. There is no trace of a path so walk in the direction of a scattered group of white stones on the slope of the hill on the right. Further up the hill, a path will be seen which will lead to a well-made cairn. Continue over the ridge to another cairn and go up the hill, keeping beside the burn as far as possible. As there is no path it is necessary to walk through the heather to the loch. The return journey is very much easier. Keep as far as possible to the many grassy areas beside the burn. Further down on the left hand side of the burn, a path will be seen which goes to the bridge.

Geology: This loch, is a kettle hole, and was formed as a result of a large block of ice being lodged in a hollow and remaining when the glacier retreated. The hills surrounding the loch are composed of granite with a small strata of dolomitic limestone in the hill to the south of the loch. It is this strata that provides the nutrients for the plants around the loch and in the burn which lodged in a hollow and remained when the glacier retreated.

Flowers: Chickweed Wintergreen, Dwarf Birch, Bog Bilberry, Bell Heather, Cross-leaved Heath, Common Dog Violet, Heath Bedstraw, Alpine Lady's Mantle, Cloudberry, Cranberry (Cowberry). Bog Asphodel, Milkwort, Rosebay Willowherb, Tormentil, Heath Spotted Orchid, Dwarf Birch, Wintergreen Intermediate Pyrola can be seen in the burn side.

Club Mosses: Fir 1,300m, Alpine 1,200m, Stags Horn 840m, Interrupted 1,000m, maximum height of growth.

Mosses: Sphagnums Capillifolium and Palustre, Philonotis Fontana, Polytrichum Commune.

Lichens: Ochrolechia Frigida, Ochrolechia Tartarea, Thamnolia Vermicularis, Cladonia Rangiferina (Reindeer Moss), Flavocetraria Nivalis.

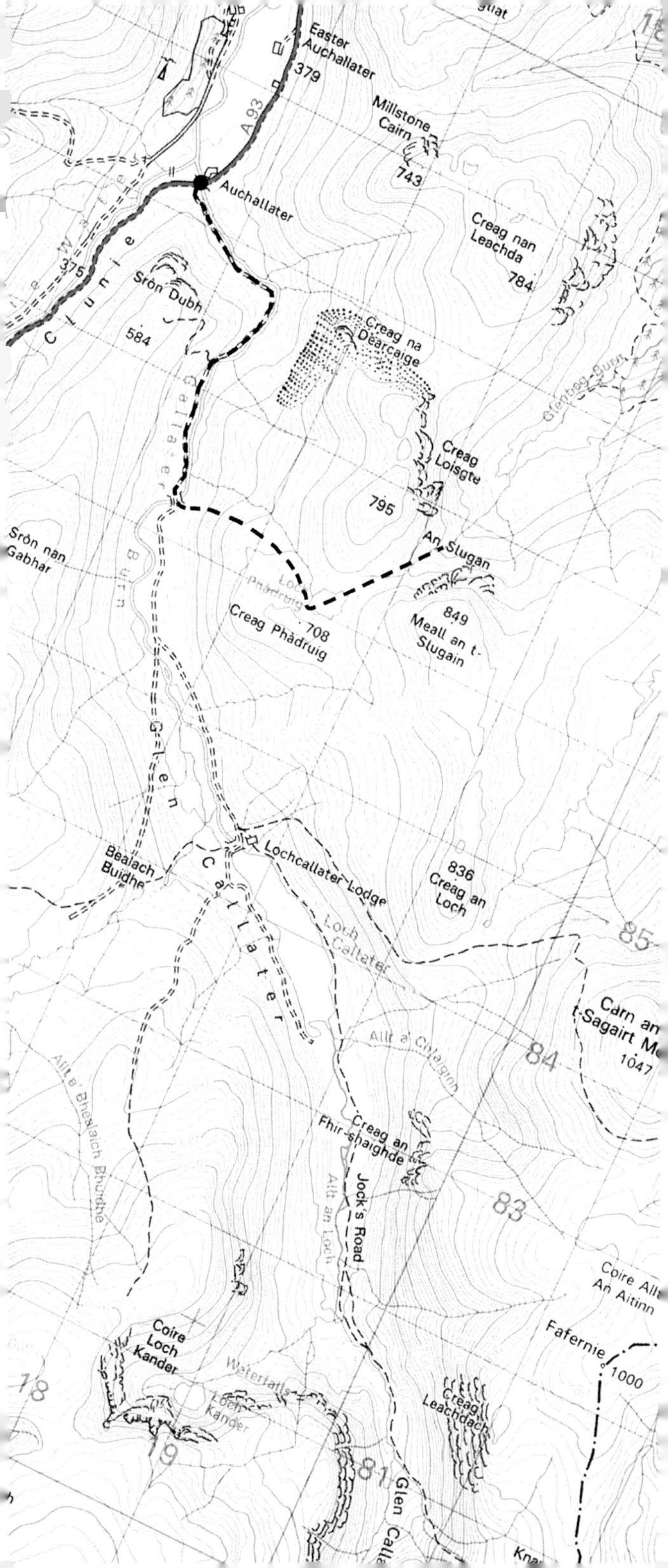
Easter Auchallater
379
A93
Millstone Cairn
743
Auchallater
Creag nan Leachda
784
375
Clunie Water
Sròn Dubh
584
Creag na Dearcaige
Glenbeg Burn
Callater Burn
Creag Loisgte
795
An Slugan
Sròn nan Gabhar
Loch Phàdruig
708
Creag Phàdruig
849
Meall an t-Slugain
Glen Callater
Bealach Buidhe
Lochcallater Lodge
836
Creag an Loch
85
Loch Callater
Carn an t-Sagairt M
1047
84
Allt a' Chlaiginn
Allt a' Bhealaich Bhuidhe
Creag an Fhir-shaighde
83
Allt an Loch
Jock's Road
Coire Allt An Aitinn
Fafernie
1000
Coire Loch Kander
Waterfalls
Loch Kander
78
79
81
Creag Leachdach
Glen Calla

9. POLL BHAT (THE POOL OF THE DROWNING) LANDRANGER MAP 43

This lochan is situated on the southern slope of Beinn Bhreac which is overlooked by Beinn a' Bhuird. It is an isolated area close to the Dubh Ghleann and a stand of old pine. As the area is rarely visited, there is a good chance of seeing wildlife. This could be a circular walk by continuing past the lochan and taking a path which descends down through the trees to Glen Derry. This is better done with two cars to save the long walk back to Allanaquoich. (Boots essential).

16 km 4 hrs net ht 236 m

Access: From Braemar take the Linn of Dee road and go down the other side of the Dee to the parking space at Allanaquoich (Grid Ref 119 912), which is the starting point for the walk.

Route: Follow the track going up the west side of the quoich to its junction with Allt an Dubh-ghlinne. On the west side of the burn there is a rough overgrown track which continues alongside the burn until it leaves the trees. It then goes onto moorland where a path is met which goes uphill to a point opposite the Poll Bhat. Go through the heather to the loch. Return by the same route.

Geology: The Poll Bhat is a kettle hole formed after the glacier which moved from Glen Derry to the quoich retreated, leaving behind a large block of ice in a hollow. The small area in which it is situated was a meltwater channel which is not in the same scale as nearby Clais Fhearnaig. The underlying rock is quartzite a hard metamorphic rock which provides little nutrient for plants.

Archaeology: The area at the mouth of the Dubh Ghleann is the site of two shielings. One reason why there is good soil in an area composed of quartzite may have been that the soil and calcareous rocks were deposited by glacial action and avoided being eroded.

Flowers: Marsh Thistle, Chickweed Wintergreen, Heath Bedstraw, Harebell, Heather, Bell Heather, Cross-leaved Heath, Rosebay Willowherb, Tormentil, Blaeberry, Milkwort, Lousewort, Cat's Ears, Hare's Tail Cotton Grass, Bog Asphodel, Starry Saxifrage, Cranberry (Cowberry), Crowberry, Cloudberry.

Club Mosses: Fir 1,300m, Alpine 1,200m, Stags Horn 840m, Interrupted 1,000m, maximum height of growth.

Mosses: Sphagnums Capillifolium and Palustre, Philonotis Fontana, Polytrichum Commune.

Lichens: Ochrolechia Frigida, Ochrolechia Tartarea, Thamnolia Vermicularis, Cladonia Rangiferina (Reindeer Moss), Flavocetraria Nivalis.

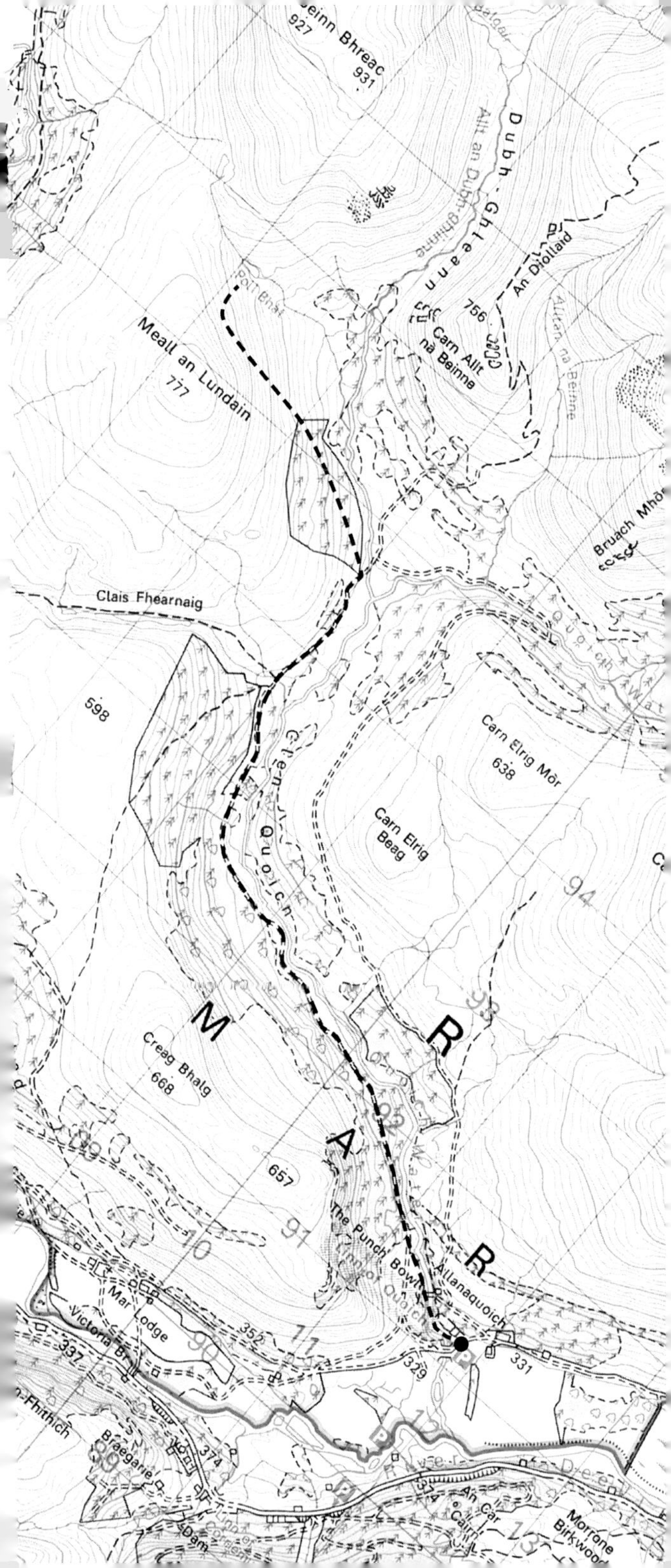

Beinn Bhreac
927
931
Dubh Ghleann
Allt an Dubh-ghlinne
An Diollaid
756
Carn Allt na Beinne
Alltan na Beinne
Poll Bhat
Meall an Lundain
777
Bruach Mhòr
Clais Fhearnaig
Quoich
598
Glen Quoich
Carn Elrig Mòr
638
Carn Elrig Beag
M
A
R
R
Creag Bhalg
668
657
The Punch Bowl
Allanaquoich
Mar Lodge
Victoria Br
352
337
329
331
374
Braegarie
An Car
Morrone Birkwood
Dam
Dee

10. CARN NA DROCHAIDE (HILL OF THE BRIDGE) LANDRANGER MAP 43

Carn na Drochaide, classed as a Corbett, is well known as a viewpoint for Beinn a' Bhuird, the hills around Braemar and the Glen Ey hills. An easy climb with a good track. Boots required in wet weather as there are two small fords. This walk is best done in late spring and autumn when the snow is on the hills and the track is clear.

12 km 3 hrs net ht 490 m

Access: From Braemar take the Linn of Dee road and go down the other side of the Dee to the parking space at Allanaquoich (Grid Ref 119 912) which is the starting point for the walk.

Route: The path starts at the Linn of Quoich and goes past the cottage, through the wood where it joins a track. Turn left and go up the hill to a stand of trees and take the track which goes uphill. This is an old, well used track which leads to Carn na Criche. Ignore any other path or tracks which go through the heather. The track goes up to Carn na Criche and continues along the broad ridge to the foot of the summit. The ground, although now more stony, presents no difficulty and it is an easy walk to the summit and the various view points. Walkers may return to the car, either by returning by the same route (1½ hrs), or by going down the east side directly to Allanaquoich. The ground is stony below the summit until it reaches short heather and a path can be picked up which leads back to the car park (1 hr 10 mins).

Geology: Carn na Drochaide and the hills on either side are all composed of quartzite which is a hard white rock comprised of metamorphised sandstone. Beinn a' Bhuird and Ben A'an which stand to the north west of Carn na Drochaide are composed of granite.

Flowers: Marsh Thistle, Chickweed Wintergreen, Harebell, Bitter Vetch, Tormentil, Devil's-bit Scabious, Blaeberry, Cranberry (Cowberry), Thyme, Heath Bedstraw, Bog Asphodel, Cross-leaved Heath, Butterwort, Hare's Tail Cotton Grass, Spotted Orchid, Bell Heather.

Club Mosses: Fir 1,300m, Alpine 1,200m, Stags Horn 840m, Interrupted 1,000m, maximum height of growth.

Mosses: Sphagnums Capillifolium and Palustre, Philonotis Fontana, Polytrichum Commune.

Lichens: Ochrolechia Frigida, Ochrolechia Tartarea, Thamnolia Vermicularis, Cladonia Rangiferina (Reindeer Moss), Flavocetraria Nivalis.

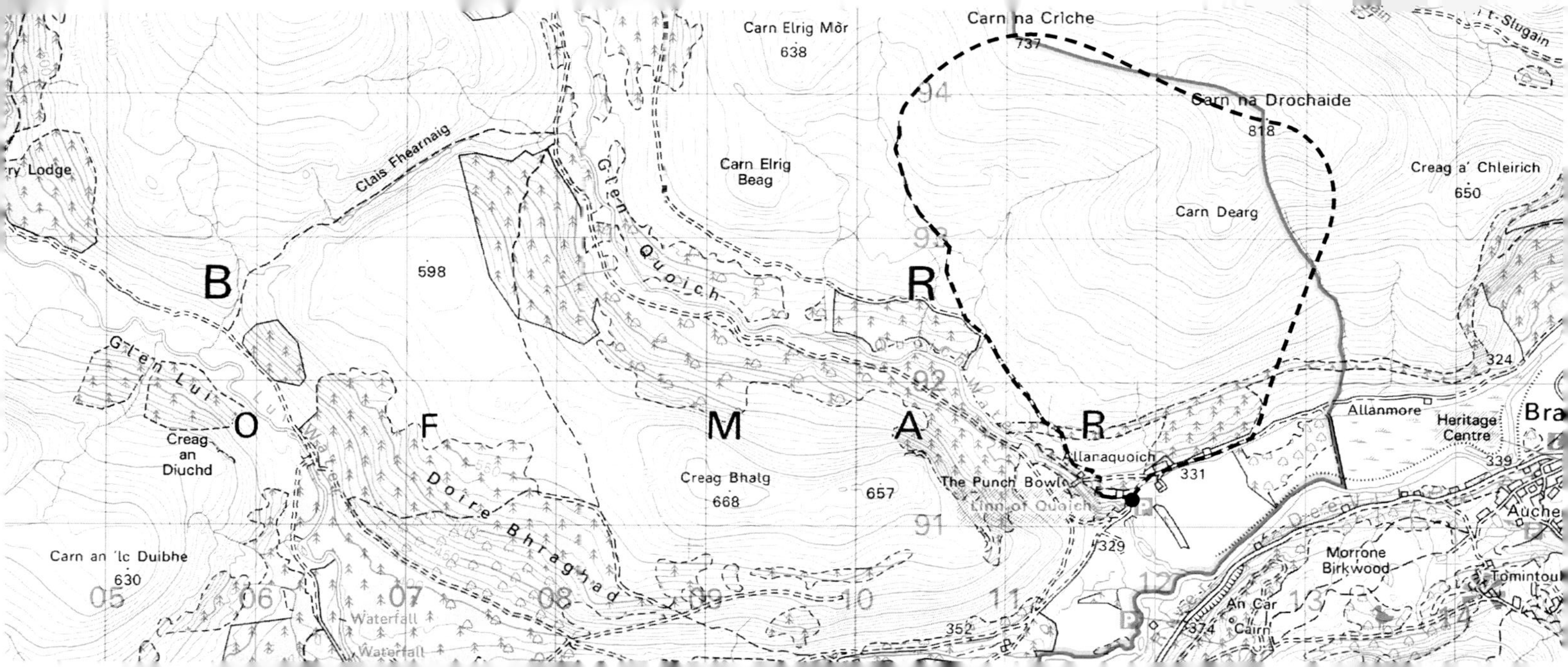
Carn na Criche
737
Carn Elrig Mòr
638
Carn na Drochaide
818
Creag a' Chleirich
650
Carn Dearg
Carn Elrig
Beag
Clais Fhearnaig
Glen Quoich
598
B
R
O
F
M
A
R
Glen Lui
Creag
an
Diuchd
Doire Bhraghad
Creag Bhalg
668
657
The Punch Bowl
Linn of Quoich
Allanaquoich
331
329
Allanmore
Heritage
Centre
339
324
Morrone
Birkwood
An Car
Cairn
374
352
Carn an 'Ic Duibhe
630
Waterfall
Waterfall
05
06
07
08
09
10
11
12
13
91
92
93
94

11. MORRONE BIRKWOOD AND TOM ANTHON LANDRANGER MAP 43

This walk passes through two different areas. The first part of the walk goes through Morrone Birkwood which contains a diverse range of plants, flowers, mosses and lichens, due to an underlying strata of limestone. Records show that the present flora has survived practically unchanged since the early post-glacial period some 12,500 years ago. It is also the best example of sub alpine birch and juniper woodland in Britain. The second area lies to the west and goes over the hill to Corriemulzie, goes around Tom Anthon in Glen Ey returning to Corriemulzie and then goes over the shoulder of Morrone to Braemar.

15 km 4½ hrs net ht 200 m

Access: This walk starts at the car park at the top of Chapel Brae in Braemar. The entrance to the Chapel Brae is at the small roundabout beside the Games Park.

Route: This walk climbs up to the viewpoint and then goes through the birks along the side of Morrone into moorland where it meets a deer fence (30 mins). Cross the stile and descend through the trees to another stile and then onto the Linn of Dee road (20 mins). Walk along this road and turn up a track beside a wood. *Go through the gate and continue through the wood to where it meets the track which goes up Glen Ey (30 mins). Take the left hand track and climb up to a col (small pass) (45 mins) and turn and descend down it. The path is a little difficult to follow so keep well up from the burn until the path reappears on the left further down. Where the path joins the Corriemulzie Burn, go up the burn a short distance to where the remains of an old lime kiln can be seen. Return to the original path which now goes up through the trees and onto a field where it meets a good track which leads to the road (35 mins) and then return to the stile (15 mins). After crossing the stile go up the track on the right, ignore a track which goes uphill, and take the track which looks overgrown but rapidly improves. The track now crosses a shallow burn and climbs up to a stile (20 mins). Go along the path beside the fence through the moor to a gate and the track which goes to the car park (30 mins).

Geology: The base of Morrone at the side facing the Dee has a strata of dolomitic limestone which being a calcareous rock gives nutrients for plants. This strata goes as far as Corriemulzie, which is also noted for its range of plants, and the foot of the small col which lies between Tom Anthon and Carn Mor.

Flowers: Bell Heather, Cross-leaved Heath, Yellow Saxifrage, Common Dog Violet, Alpine Cinquefoil, Golden Saxifrage, Coltsfoot, Common Rockrose, Mountain Pansy, Mountain Everlasting, Germander Speedwell, Eyebright, Bog Asphodel, Yellow Mountain Saxifrage, Thyme, Field Gentian, Hare's Tail Cotton Grass.

Club Mosses: Fir 1,300m, Alpine 1,200m, Stags Horn 840m, Interrupted 1,000m, maximum height of growth.

Mosses: Sphagnums Capillifolium and Palustre, Philonotis Fontana, Polytrichum Commune.

Lichens: Ochrolechia Frigida, Ochrolechia Tartarea, Thamnolia Vermicularis, Cladonia Rangiferina (Reindeer Moss), Flavocetraria Nivalis.

*Note: From this point, use the map for walk 7.

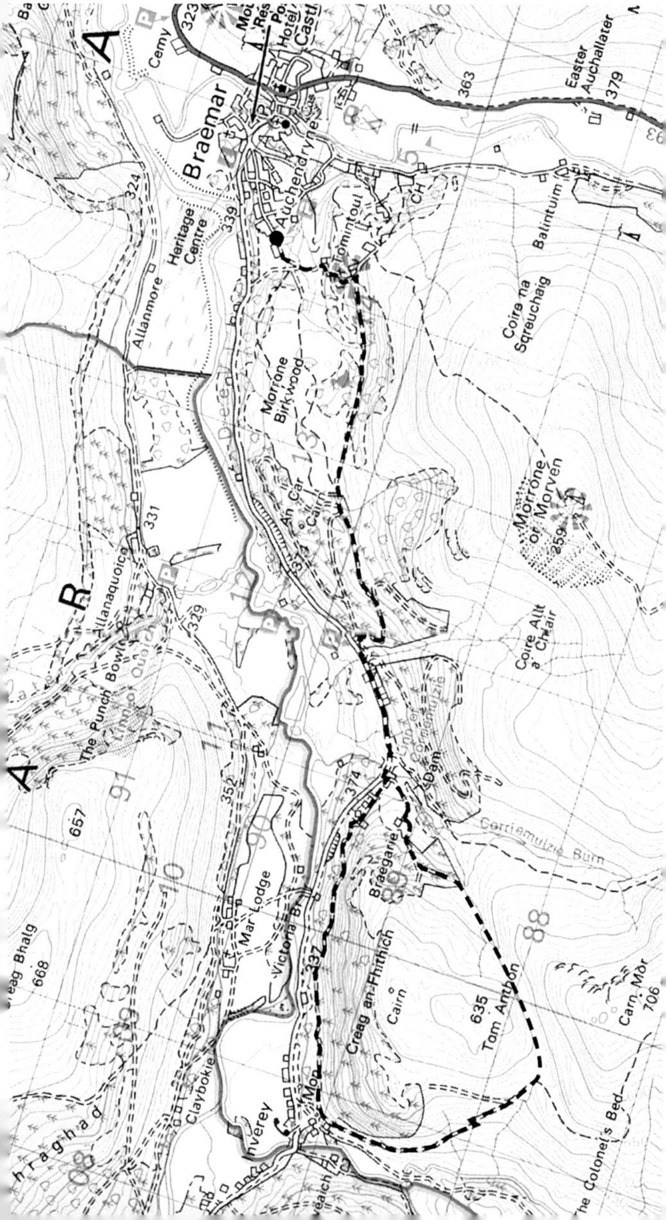

12. CAPEL MOUNTH LANDRANGER MAP 44

A walk which goes from Spittal of Muick to Glen Clova which apart from the climb up the shoulder of Black Hill is mainly over moorland. The journey is dangerous in winter, as it is very exposed and cairns were erected to guide early travellers. There are good views of Lochnagar and surrounding hills, best seen in the late spring when the snow is still on the hills.

12 km 3 hrs net ht 280 m

Access: The road to Loch Muick starts at Bridge of Muick which is on the B926. There is good parking (£3 parking fee) and toilet facilities.

Route: Start on the track which goes round the loch and turn up the track which branches up the hill on the left. The track goes up the hill for 2½ km before it levels off and then continues on moorland to Glen Clova. For those wishing a shorter walk turn at the second burn.

Geology: The underlying rock on the walk is quartzite and granite and therefore there are limited nutrients for plants. Loch Muick was formed as a result of the glaciers remaining on the upper part of the glen for a longer period as it was sheltered from the sun and the area was subjected to more erosion, which lowered the level of the ground.

Archaeology: A "rickle of stanes" on the roadside before reaching the car park are all that remains of two long houses (around 1000 years old). This was the site of a farm called Titaboutie, which was also an ale house and the drovers intending to go over the Capel Mounth rested and slept in barns at the farm. The ale house moved to the Spittal in 1815. At the foot of the Darrarie Burn there are mounds and cairns of men and women who died when crossing the Mounth Road in winter.

Flowers: Heather, Crowberry, Blaeberry, Cranberry (Cowberry), Cloudberry, Alpine Lady's Mantle, Butterwort, Bog Asphodel, Bird's Foot Trefoil, Bell Heather, Eyebright, Whin, Heath, Milkwort, Lousewort, Tormentil, Thyme, Chickweed Wintergreen, Cross-leaved Heath, Creeping Azaleas, Starry Saxifrage, Hare's Tail Cotton Grass.

Club Mosses: Fir 1,300m, Alpine 1,200m, Stags Horn 840m, Interrupted 1,000m, maximum height of growth.

Mosses: Sphagnums Capillifolium and Palustre, Philonotis Fontana, Polytrichum Commune.

Lichens: Ochrolechia Frigida, Ochrolechia Tartarea, Thamnolia Vermicularis, Cladonia Rangiferina (Reindeer Moss), Flavocetraria Nivalis.

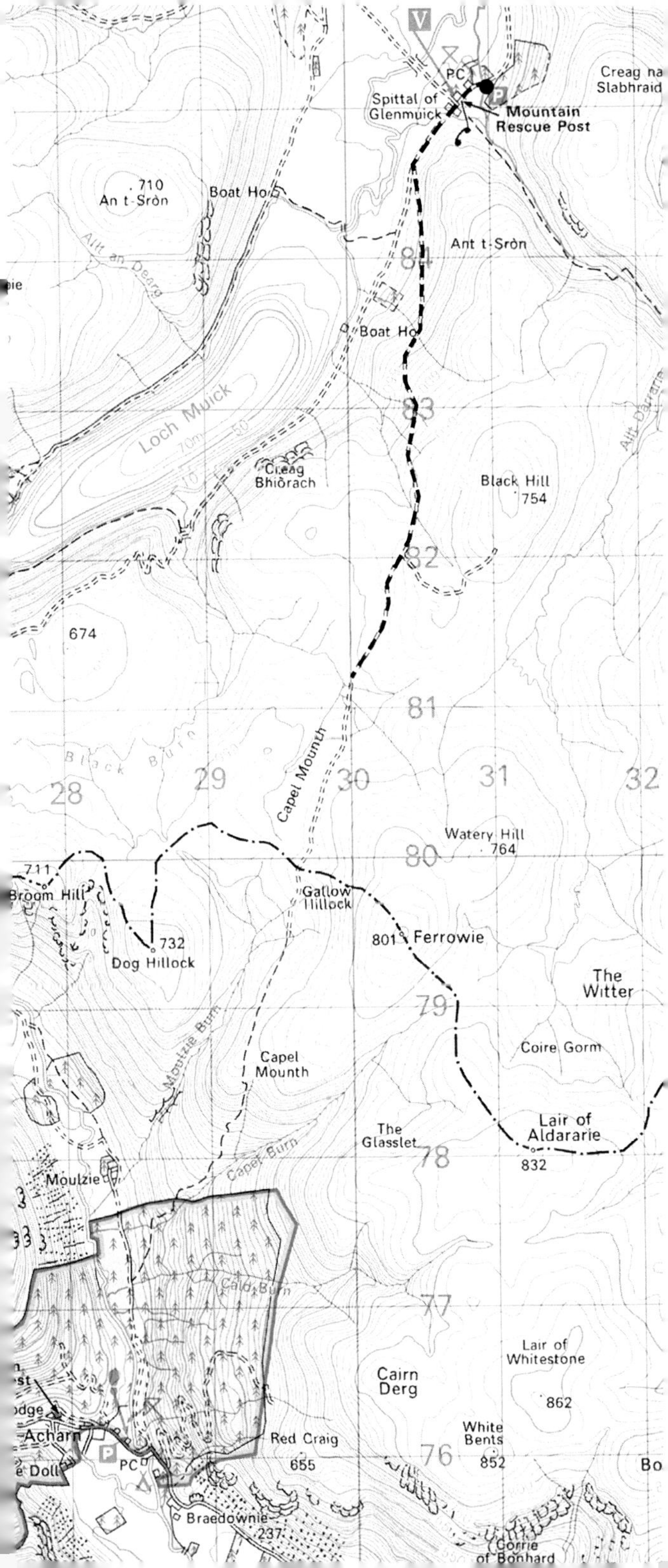

Creag na Slabhraid
PC
Spittal of Glenmuick
Mountain Rescue Post
710
An t-Sròn
Boat Ho
Ant t-Sròn
Allt an Dearg
84
Boat Ho
Loch Muick
83
Creag Bhiòrach
Black Hill
754
82
674
81
Black Burn
Capel Mounth
28
29
30
31
32
Watery Hill
764
80
711
Broom Hill
Gallow Hillock
732
Dog Hillock
801
Ferrowie
The Witter
79
Moulzie Burn
Capel Mounth
Coire Gorm
Lair of Aldararie
The Glasslet
78
832
Capel Burn
Moulzie
Cald Burn
77
Lair of Whitestone
Cairn Derg
862
White Bents
Red Craig
Acharn
PC
655
76
852
Doll
Braedownie
237
Corrie of Bonhard

13. THE COYLES OF MUICK LANDRANGER MAP 44

This walk to the three hills called the Coyles of Muick, gives good views of Glen Muïck, Glen Girnock and Lochnagar. It is frequently visited by botanists as it is a Site of Special Scientific Interest, due to the variety of flowers which grow on the upper part of these hills. The Ordnance Survey map incorrectly names only one hill as the Coyles when the term should be applied to the hills called Meall Dubh, Craig of Loinmuie and the Coyles of Muick.

10 km 3 hrs net ht 360 m

Access: From Ballater, cross the bridge to the B976 and turn right. Cross the Bridge of Muick and take an unmarked road on the left, which is a kilometre from the bridge. There is a small post box at the entrance. One kilometre from this entrance there is a parking site on the right just past a bridge with railings (Grid Ref 348 435).

Route: Start at the track which goes up through the wood towards the hill on the skyline. The track leaves the wood and goes round a large open area which is on the left. Continue on to a junction with another track which goes uphill. Thirty minutes from this junction there is another junction, this time with a rough track. This goes through the wood, past a large hut, where it meets the track which goes along the ridge between the Coyles and Craig of Loinmuie. The climb to the summit of the Coyle will take 15 minutes.

Geology: The summits of these three hills are composed of serpentinite, a rock containing magnesium which erodes easily and provides magnesium essential for growth of plants.

Flowers: Common Cow Wheat, Chickweed Wintergreen, Eyebright, Field Gentian, Heath Bedstraw, Mossy Saxifrage, Starry Saxifrage, Yellow Saxifrage, Thrift, St John's Wort, Wood Anemone, Mountain Everlasting, Fragrant Orchid, Common Spotted Orchid, Germander Speedwell, Marsh Thistle, Alpine Mouse-ear, Heathers and Heaths, Blaeberry, Cranberry (Cowberry), Hare's Tail Cotton Grass.

Club Mosses: Fir 1,300m, Alpine 1,200m, Stags Horn 840m, Interrupted 1,000m, maximum height of growth.

Mosses: Sphagnums Capillifolium and Palustre, Philonotis Fontana, Polytrichum Commune.

Lichens: Ochrolechia Frigida, Ochrolechia Tartarea, Thamnolia Vermicularis, Cladonia Rangiferina (Reindeer Moss), Flavocetraria Nivalis.

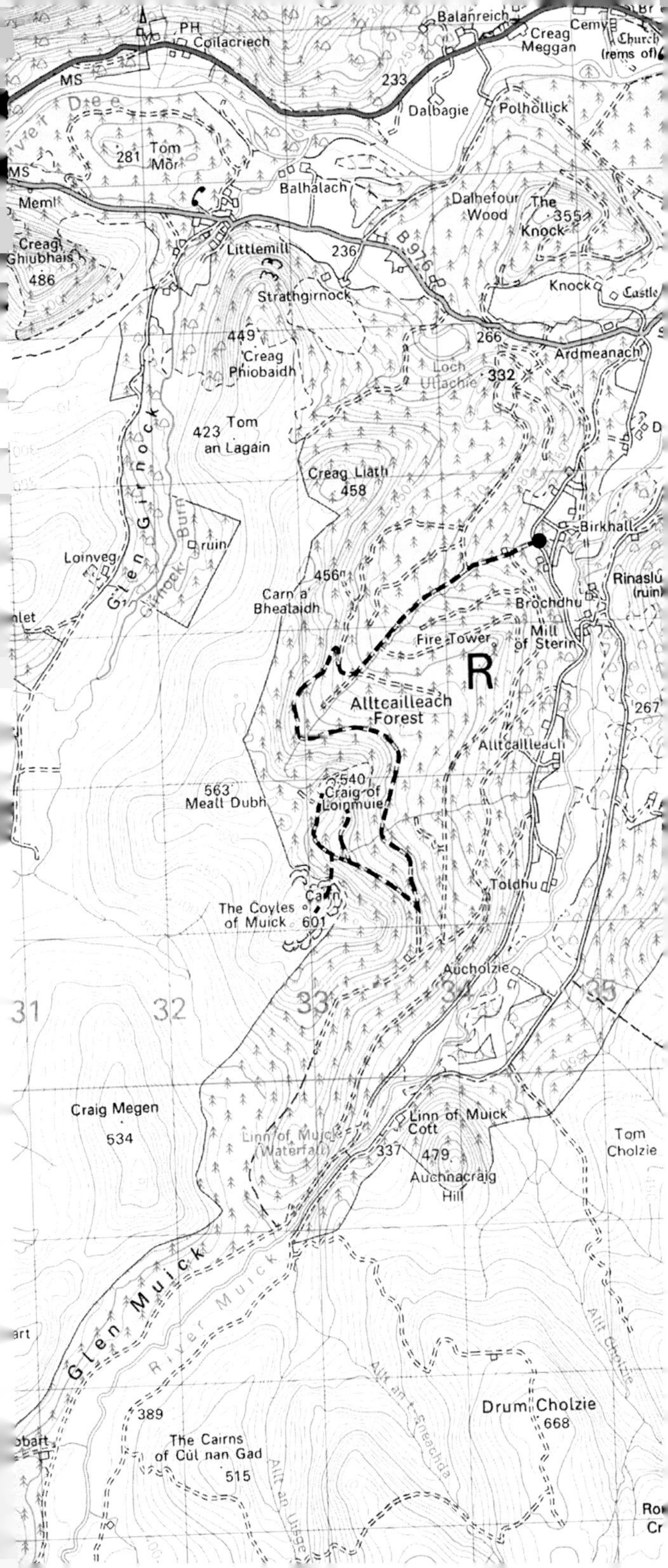

PH
Coilacriech
Balanreich
Creag Meggan
Cemy
Church (rems of)
MS
233
Dalbagie
Polhollick
281 Tom Mòr
MS
Balhalach
Meml
Dalhefour Wood
The Knock
355
Creag Ghiubhais
486
Littlemill
236
B976
Knock
Castle
Strathgirnock
449
Creag Phiobaidh
266
Ardmeanach
Loch Ullachie
332
423 Tom an Lagain
Glen Girnock
Creag Liath
458
Birkhall
Loinveg
ruin
Girnock Burn
456
Rinaslú (ruin)
Carn a' Bhealaidh
Brochdhu
Mill of Sterin
Fire Tower
R
Alltcailleach Forest
267
Alltcailleach
540
Craig of Loinmuie
563
Meall Dubh
Toldhu
Cairn
The Coyles of Muick
601
Aucholzie
31
32
33
34
35
Craig Megen
534
Linn of Muick Cott
Linn of Muick (Waterfall)
337
479
Auchnacraig Hill
Tom Cholzie
Glen Muick
River Muick
Allt an t-Sneachda
Allt Cholzie
389
Drum Cholzie
668
The Cairns of Cùl nan Gad
515
Allt an Uisge

14. CAIRN LEUCHAN (HILL OF THE WET SPOTS) LANDRANGER MAP 44

Cairn Leuchan is at the northern end of a range of peaks all about 700 m in height which are on the rim of hills overlooking the lower part of Glen Gairn. To the east of the ridge there is moorland which stretches back to the hills on the north side of Glen Tanar. It is an easy hill to climb and is an excellent vantage point to see Lochnagar, Glen Muick, Morven and the lower Deeside hills.

17 km 3 hrs net ht 490 m

Access: From Ballater, cross the Bridge to the B976 and stop at the small "field" on the right just before the Bridge of Muick which can be used for parking the car. If coming from the west, cross the Bridge of Muick and park at the small field on the left (Grid Ref 367 948).

Route: A track will be seen on the left of the road going to Glen Muick which goes through trees for a kilometre before it reaches the heather-clad slope of Craig Vallich (Rocky Hill of the Pass). It continues up the hill to a ridge and then ascends a gentle slope to Cairn Leuchan. The return is by the same route.

Geology: The summit of the hill is situated in the rim of Glen Muick and it is reasonable to assume that the present hill was part of a hill which was truncated by the glaciers coming down Glen Muick. The underlying rock of this hill is gneiss and sempelite which are metamorphic rocks and so provide limited nutrients for plants.

Flowers: Heather, Bell Heather, Crowberry, Cranberry (Cowberry), Blaeberry, Cloudberry, Alpine Lady's Mantle, Butterwort, Bog Asphodel, Bird's Foot Trefoil, Heath Bedstraw, Heath Milkwort, Lousewort, Eyebright, Tormentil, Thyme, Chickweed Wintergreen, Creeping Azalea, Starry Saxifrage, Yellow Mountain Saxifrage, Hare's Tail Cotton Grass.

Club Mosses: Fir 1,300m, Alpine 1,200m, Stags Horn 840m, Interrupted 1,000m, maximum height of growth.

Mosses: Sphagnums Capillifolium and Palustre, Philonotis Fontana, Polytrichum Commune.

Lichens: Ochrolechia Frigida, Ochrolechia Tartarea, Thamnolia Vermicularis, Cladonia Rangiferina (Reindeer Moss), Flavocetraria Nivalis.

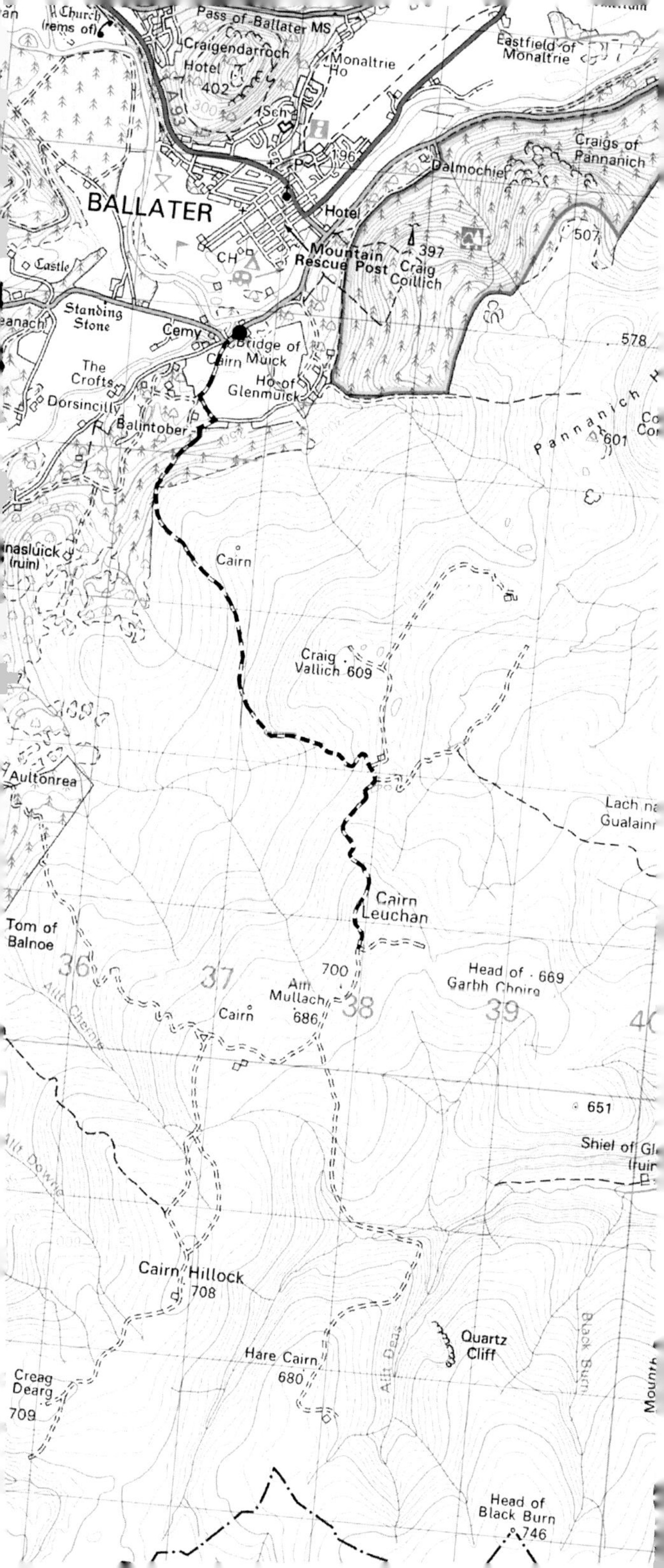
Church (rems of)
Pass of Ballater MS
Craigendarroch Hotel
402
300
A93
Monaltrie Ho
Eastfield of Monaltrie
Sch
B976
Craigs of Pannanich
Dalmochie
BALLATER
Hotel
507
Castle
CH
Mountain Rescue Post
397
Craig Coillich
Standing Stone
Cemy
Bridge of Muick
578
Cairn
The Crofts
Ho of Glenmuick
Dorsincilly
Balintober
Pannanich H
601
Cairn
Craig Vallich 609
Aultonrea
Lach na Gualainn
Cairn Leuchan
Tom of Balnoe
36
37
700
Am Mullach
686
38
Head of Garbh Choire
669
39
Cairn
Allt Cherny
651
Allt Dowie
Shiel of Gl
Cairn Hillock
708
Quartz Cliff
Hare Cairn
680
Allt Deas
Black Burn
Creag Dearg
709
Head of Black Burn
746

15. GREYSTONE, ETNACH AND DEECASTLE LANDRANGER MAP 44

The track which goes over the hills to Etnach in upper Glen Tanar is well graded and served at one time as a drove, peat and kirk road. This area covered by the walk provides a good variety of scenery from Morven and upper Glen Tanar including Mount Keen. It then continues down Glen Tanar and joins an old disused track which goes over the shoulder of Black Craig to Deecastle.

15 km 4½ hrs net ht 350 m

Access: The walk starts at Tombae Farm, Greystone, where cars can be parked (Grid Ref 435 963). The farm is a short distance from the B970.

Route: The well graded track goes up the shoulder of Craigrae Beg (Smooth Craig), where it levels out and then ascends over the shoulder of Bad na Ban (Clump of the Woman) where it descends steeply past the 18th Century settlement at Etnach and then joins the track which goes over the shoulder of Mount Keen to Angus. The route now goes down Glen Tanar past the cattle grid to a small sand pit, where whins, a small green shrub, line the track on the left hand side. *(Boots necessary when there has been a lot of rain).*

To join the track going to Deecastle, climb past the sand pit and through the trees. There is no path at the beginning and it is a little rough. The trees then open up and the going becomes very much easier and, after 15 minutes, a large track will be met. Turn left along this track to a large area in the forest and go to the far end where another track will be seen going up through the trees. This track now goes up and round the shoulder of Slai na Gour where it turns north. After leaving the trees the track goes down and through the trees lower down. Turn left when it joins another track which leads back to Greystone.

Geology: The underlying strata for the majority of this walk is granite which does not provide much nutrients for plants. When descending in Glen Tanar a large area of grass and juniper will be seen at Etnach which is in contrast to the heather-clad surrounding hills. This growth is due to a strata of calcareous schist above the settlement.

Archaeology: There is a wide variety of building remains in Etnach ranging from 17th Century to 19th Century buildings. Apart from shielings, there are remains of longhouses, enclosures for livestock, a well, a possible whisky still, a quarry and a rocking stone.

Flowers: Heather, Bell Heather, Cross-leaved Heath, Yellow Mountain Saxifrage, Whin, Intermediate Wintergreen, Cranberry (Cowberry), Blaeberry, Cloudberry, Lousewort, Eyebright, Tormentil, Starry Saxifrage, Creeping Azalea, Thyme, Bog Asphodel, Hare's Tail Cotton Grass.

Club Mosses: Fir 1,300m, Alpine 1,200m, Stags Horn 840m, Interrupted 1,000m, maximum height of growth.

Mosses: Sphagnums Capillifolium and Palustre, Philonotis Fontana, Polytrichum Commune.

Lichens: Ochrolechia Frigida, Ochrolechia Tartarea, Thamnolia Vermicularis, Cladonia Rangiferina (Reindeer Moss), Flavocetraria Nivalis.

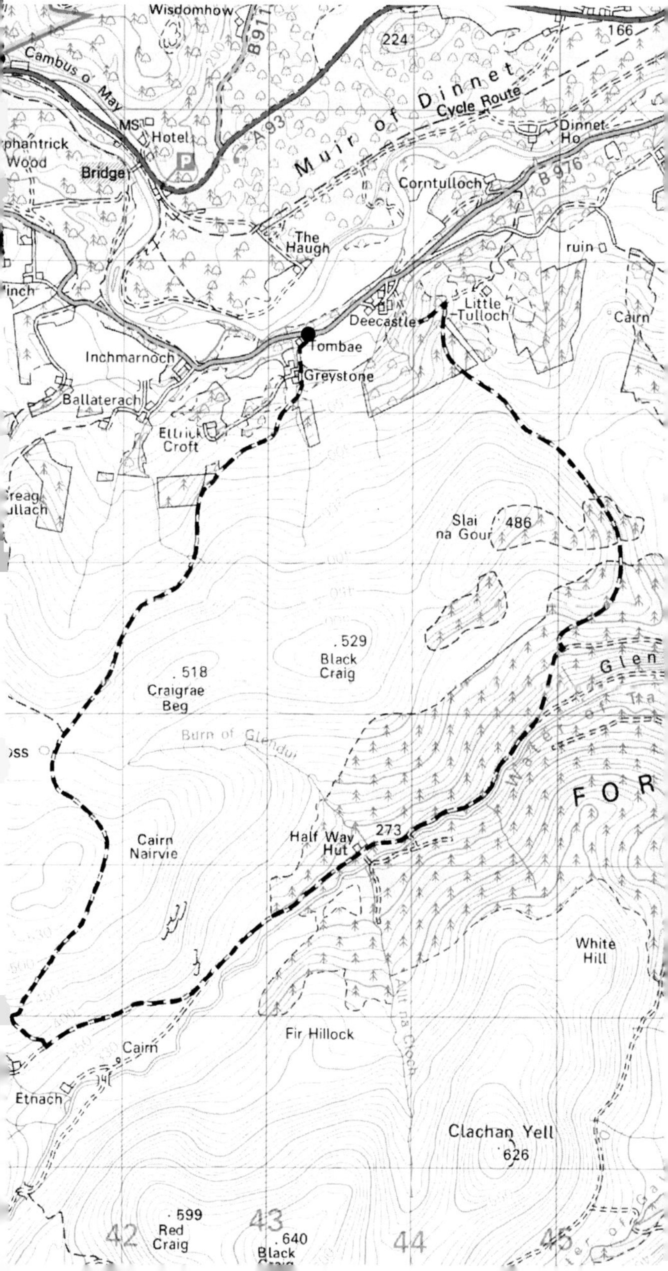

16. DEECASTLE, BLACK CRAIG AND GREYSTONE LANDRANGER MAP 44

There is a walk from Deeside over the shoulder of Tom Lair a hill on the north side of Glen Tanar. At the top of the hill turn southwards over short heather to Black Craig. On the southern end of the hill there is a track which joins the old road from Greystone to Etnach. It gives good views of Mount Keen and the Howe of Cromar. Deecastle, which was formerly the site of a hunting lodge, owned by the Earl of Aboyne, of which there is apparently no trace. Deecastle was formerly called Candakyle and the name was changed in 1815.

10 km 3 hrs net ht 336 m

Access: The starting point for this walk is at Deecastle Farm where cars can be parked. The farm is a short distance from the B970, 6¼ km from Dinnet Bridge (Grid Ref 439 967).

Route: Go through a gate to the east of the house which gives access to a track which climbs steeply as far as a dyke where a grassed bank is seen going through the woods on the right. Continue on this track through the wood and then onto moorland for 2 km to a plantation of fir trees. Take the second heather track on the right which goes up through the trees to the cairn on top of Slai na Gour and continue in the direction of Black Craig. There is an overgrown track which can be followed which goes over a large flat area of short heather to the foot of Black Craig. This track descends to Glen Tanar, so leave it, and go up and over Black Craig and Craigrae Beg, where a path will be picked up leading to the track from Greystone to Glen Tanar. Turn right at the junction to go down to Greystone and then to Deecastle (1 hr).

Geology: The walk begins by going through farmland which contains calcareous rock and for the rest of the walk the underlying strata is granite so the range of plant life is limited. The granite base of Greystone Hill ensured that it could withstand the erosion from the glacier which went down Glen Tanar.

Flowers: Heather, Bell Heather, Cross-leaved Heath, Yellow Mountain Saxifrage, Whin, Intermediate Wintergreen, Blaeberry, Cranberry (Cowberry), Alpine Lady's Mantle, Lousewort, Tormentil, Thyme, Bog Asphodel, Butterwort, Hare's Tail Cotton Grass.

Club Mosses: Fir 1,300m, Alpine 1,200m, Stags Horn 840m, Interrupted 1,000m, maximum height of growth.

Mosses: Sphagnums Capillifolium and Palustre, Philonotis Fontana, Polytrichum Commune.

Lichens: Ochrolechia Frigida, Ochrolechia Tartarea, Thamnolia Vermicularis, Cladonia Rangiferina (Reindeer Moss), Flavocetraria Nivalis.

Bog
dismtd rly
Sawmill
St James's
Glen Tanar Church
Cobbleheugh
Meml
Burnroot
Mill of Dinnet
Stone
Candycraig
Belrorie Hill
284
Kildhu
243
Millfield
Belrorie
Fasnadarach
152
Burnside
Dinnet
B 9158
Oldhall
Cairn
Tillycairn
Hillhead
Glen Tanar Ho
260
Home Farm
Weir
Netherton
Newton
166
Dinnet Ho
B 976
ruin
Cairn
406
Creag na Slice
Little Tulloch
Deecastle
Tombae
Greystone
Slai na Gour
486
Glen Tanar
Water of Tanar
FOREST
Ettrick Croft
529
Black Craig
273
Half Way Hut
518
Craigrae Beg
Burn of Glendui
Allt na Croe
Fir Hillock
Cairn Nairvie
Rocking Stone
Black Moss
Cairn
599
Red Craig
93
606
Knockie Branar
Etnach
92
42

17. GLEN TANAR, GLEN GAIRNEY AND ETNACH (THE PLACE OF THE JUNIPERS) LANDRANGER MAP 44

The majority of walkers who go to Glen Tanar follow the Tanar and the Allachy Burn and therefore have only a limited view of the surrounding hills. This walk does provide views of upper Glen Tanar by going up Glen Gairney, a small glen which is situated in the middle of the Glen Tanar. It then continues round Black and Red Craig where there is a choice of two routes for the return journey. There is also the opportunity to visit a settlement which has been inhabited since the 17th Century.

Route a) 22 km 5 hrs net ht 300 m
Route b) 25 km 6 hrs net ht 300 m

Access: The entrance to Glen Tanar from Aboyne is 2½ km past Aboyne bridge on the B976. From Ballater take the B993 to Dinnet, cross the bridge to the B976 for 5 km to the entrance for Glen Tanar. The starting point of the walk is at the car park (Grid Ref 480 968), which is 2½ km from the entrance to the glen. There is a charge of £2 for the use of the car park and toilet facilities are available over the bridge on the left.

Route: Go over the bridge, past the church and take the track which goes up beside the Tanar Burn and turn right at the second bridge and take the first track on the left which goes up Glen Gairney. This goes steeply up through the trees and then enters moorland. The route then goes alongside Clachan Yell (Hill of the White Stones) and goes over the slopes of Black and Red Craig and then on to the bridge over the Tanar. The old settlement of Etnach (Grid Ref 466 938), is a short distance down the track. At this point, walkers have a choice of a) continuing down through the trees, alongside the Tanar and then back to the car, or b) returning by the original route down through the old Scots pines in Glen Gairney, to the track which goes to the second bridge and then back to the car.

Geology: The underlying rock of the hills in upper Glen Tanar is granite, a rock which is resistant to normal erosion. There is no calcareous rock in the area to provide nutrients for plants, so the range of flowers to be seen is limited. *(See comment on the calcareous rock around Etnach in Walk 15).* These granite hills were able to withstand, to some extent, the action of chemical weathering and later glaciation.

Flowers: Heather, Bell Heather, Blaeberry, Crowberry (Bearberry), Cranberry (Cowberry), Bog Asphodel, Bearberry (on White Hill), Cross-leaved Heath, Thyme, Butterwort, Lousewort, Hare's Tail Cotton Grass.

Club Mosses: Fir 1,300m, Alpine 1,200m, Stags Horn 840m, Interrupted 1,000m, maximum height of growth.

Mosses: Sphagnums Capillifolium and Palustre, Philonotis Fontana, Polytrichum Commune.

Lichens: Refer to Walk 16.

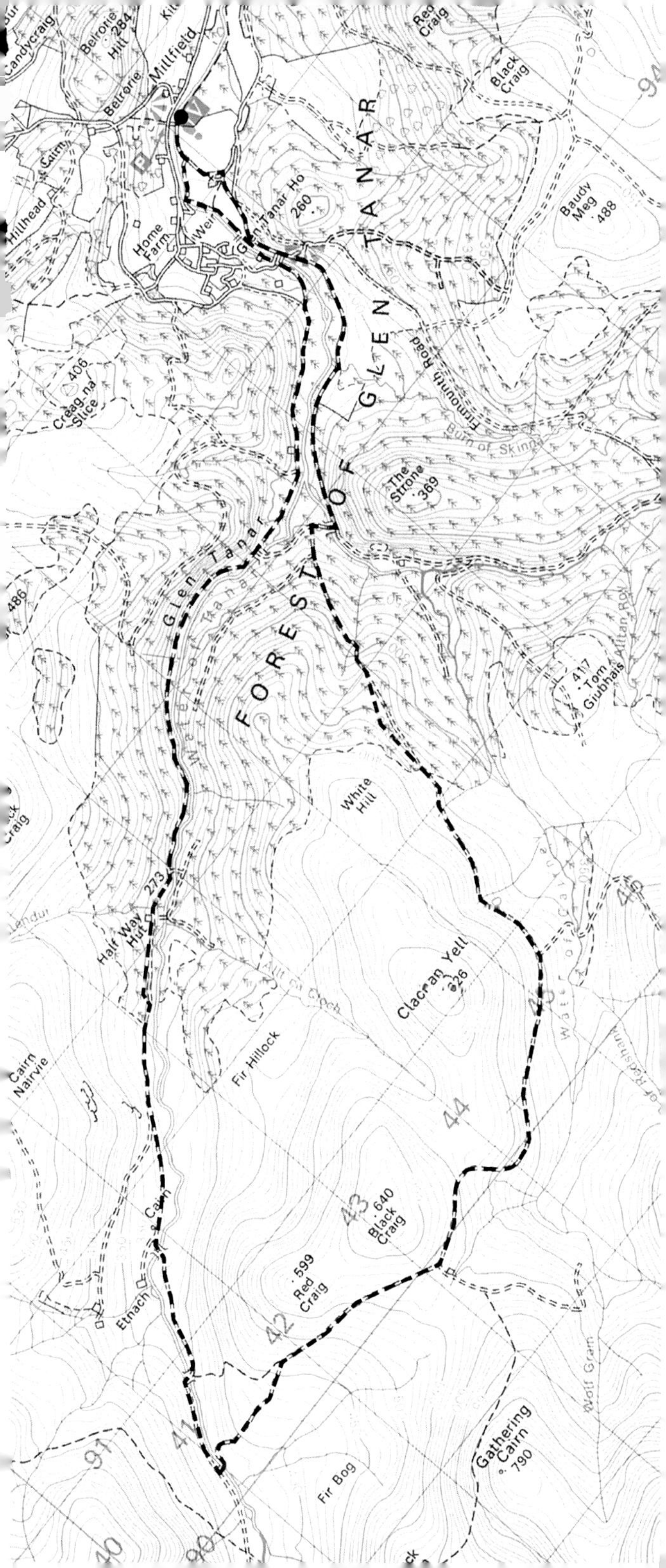

Candycraig
Belrorie Hill 284
Millfield
Belrorie
Red Craig
Black Craig
Cairn
Hillhead
Home Farm
Weir
Glen Tanar Ho
260
FOREST OF GLEN TANAR
Baudy Meg 488
Firmounth Road
Burn of Skinna
The Strone 369
406 Creag na Slice
486
Glen Tanar
Water of Tanar
417 Tom Giubhais
White Hill
273
Half Way Hut
Fir Hillock
Cairn Nairvie
640 Black Craig
599 Red Craig
Etnach
Fir Bog
Gathering Cairn 790
44
43
42
41

18. LARY, MORVEN LODGE AND GLEN FENZIE LANDRANGER MAP 37

A good variety of scenery is encountered on this walk which starts at the entrance to Glen Fenzie (pronounced Finnie). The path from Lary goes through a large area of grassland then climbs over Tom Liath, the hill behind Morven Lodge and descends through a small glen to Glen Fenzie. The walk is completed by going down alongside the Fenzie Burn to Lary.

11 km 4 hrs net ht 350 m

Access: The road to Lary starts at the Bridge of Gairn on the A93. It is a narrow unmarked road which climbs up the east side of Glen Gairn to Lary (2 km). There is limited car parking space – no charge.

Route: The track starts at the parking area and goes eastwards before turning northwards towards a small clump of firs which is beside the lodge. The track turns left and goes up past a ruined house and continues on the eastern shoulder of Tom Liath and then descends steeply into a small glen containing one of the two tributaries of the Fenzie Burn. At the mouth of the glen stands Glenfenzie, a deserted farm now overgrown with juniper bushes, an indication of fertile soil. Continue on this track which goes beside the burn before turning eastwards around the southern shoulder of Tom Liath.

At the highest part of this track the Ordnance Survey Map shows that there is a path down over the moor to Lary. Unfortunately this path is now overgrown. By walking through the heather which is relatively open, it is possible to reach a path which does exist lower down. From the sandpit at the top of the track, walk over the short heather to a large patch of dead heather and at the bottom left hand corner there is a small path leading to two pine trees alongside the burn. From this point, the path to Lary is a little overgrown in parts so progress is a little slow.

Geology: There is calcareous rock in the moor to the south of the lodge and more basic rock to the north of Tom Liath. There is more calcareous rock around Fenzie Farm as shown by the large amount of juniper in that area.

Flowers: Heather, Crowberry (Bearberry), Blaeberry, Chickweed Wintergreen, Dog Violet, Wood Anemone, Bog Asphodel, Butterwort, Bell Heather, Lousewort, Thyme, Cranberry (Cowberry), Hare's Tail Cotton Grass.

Club Mosses: Fir 1,300m, Alpine 1,200m, Stags Horn 840m, Interrupted 1,000m, maximum height of growth.

Mosses: Sphagnums Capillifolium and Palustre, Philonotis Fontana, Polytrichum Commune.

Lichens: Ochrolechia Frigida, Ochrolechia Tartarea, Thamnolia Vermicularis, Cladonia Rangiferina (Reindeer Moss), Flavocetraria Nivalis.

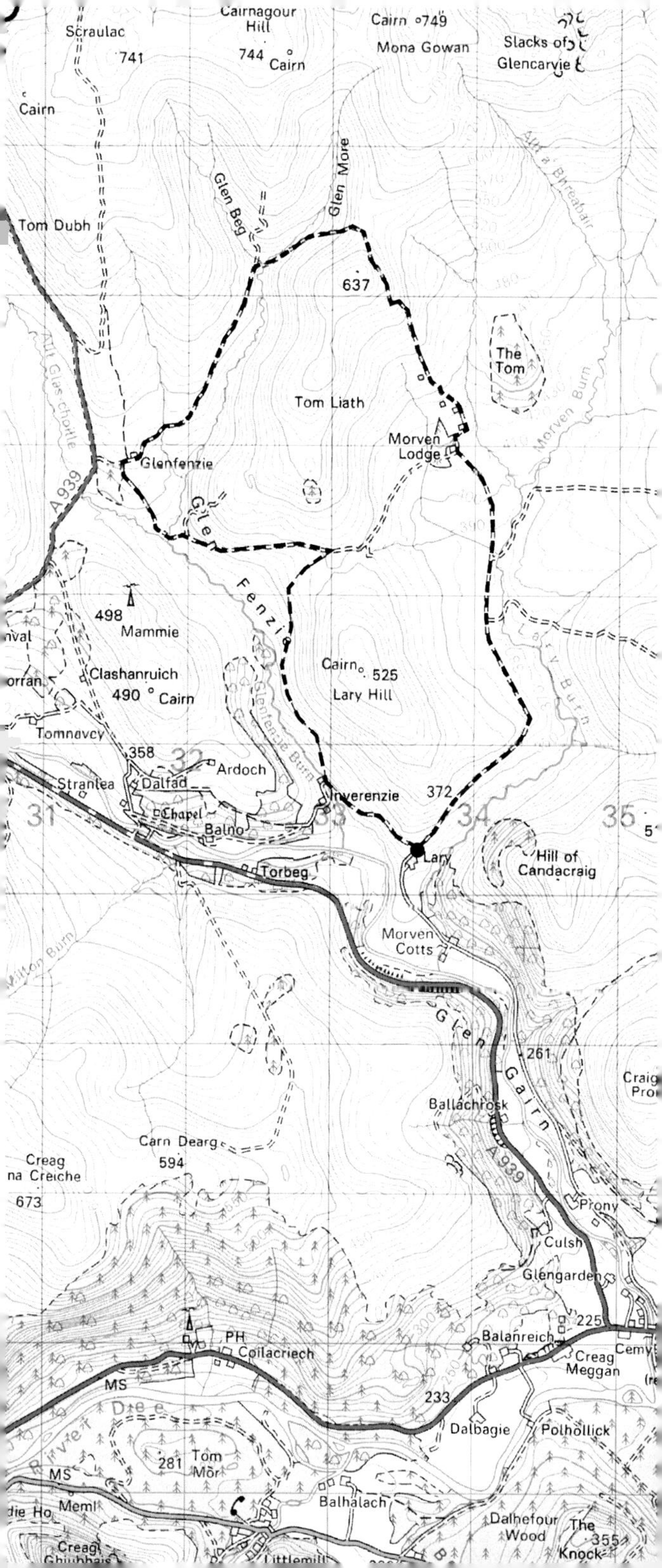

Cairnagour Hill
744 Cairn
Scraulac
741
Cairn 749
Mona Gowan
Slacks of Glencarvie
Cairn
Tom Dubh
Glen Beg
Glen More
637
The Tom
Tom Liath
Morven Lodge
Morven Burn
Glenfenzie
A939
Glen Fenzie
498
Mammie
Clashanruich
490 Cairn
Cairn 525
Lary Hill
Lary Burn
Tomnavey
358
Ardoch
Dalfad
Stranlea
Chapel
Balno
Inverenzie
372
Lary
Hill of Candacraig
Torbeg
Morven Cotts
Glen Gairn
261
Ballachrosk
Carn Dearg
594
Creag na Creiche
673
Prony
Culsh
Glengarden
225
Balanreich
Creag Meggan
PH
Coilacriech
MS
233
River Dee
Dalbagie
Polhollick
281 Tom Mòr
Balhalach
Dalhefour Wood
The Knock
355
Littlemill
31
32
33
34
35

19. CULBLEAN AND THE MUIR OF DINNET LANDRANGER MAP 37

This is a walk over the eastern Culblean (the warm hill), using an old droving road and going into the Nature Reserve at the Muir of Dinnet to examine features such as the Burn of Vat and the birds, of which there is a very wide variety during the summer. The Visitor Centre contains a considerable amount of information about the Nature Reserve and there are leaflets which describe various points of interest such as Stone Age settlements and sites where birds can be seen around the two lochs. The path to the Burn of Vat contains many flowers, mosses and lichens and the Vat itself is an interesting geological feature.

10 km 3½ hrs net ht 160 m

Access: There is a large car park at Turnerhall (Grid Ref 406 981). Turnerhall is on the A93 and is 5 km from Ballater and 6 km from Dinnet. There are toilet facilities at the Visitor Centre at the Burn of Vat.

Route: The route starts at the car park and goes up the hill to a point just before the track and turns left, where there is a post indicating a path which goes along the side of Culblean. This joins a track which continues over the hill, past a path going to the Visitor Centre and which then continues down to the B9119 (1 hr 10 mins). The path to the reserve is on the other side of the road which follows the dyke and then meets a signpost (15 mins) indicating the direction to the Burn of Vat and the Visitor Centre (45 mins). There is a path going uphill from the car park which joins the original track (30 mins), and returns to the car park at Turnerhall (30 mins).

Geology: The underlying rock for Culblean is granite which intruded in deposits of limestone and mudstone which were metamorphisised into calcareous schist. These rocks were later covered by glacial deposits. The area around the Burn of Vat was part of a meltwater channel and the Vat is an example of the force exerted by meltwater over a period of years.

Flowers: Wild Raspberry, Alpine Lady's Mantle, Golden Saxifrage, Sundew, Alpine Bistort (Culblean), Crowberry (Bearberry), Heather, Cross-leaved Heath, Cranberry (Cowberry), Primrose, Chickweed Wintergreen, Speedwell, Thyme, Ladies Bedstraw, Devil's-bit Scabious, Hare's Tail Cotton Grass.

Club Mosses: Fir 1,300m, Alpine 1,200m, Stags Horn 840m, Interrupted 1,000m, maximum height of growth.

Mosses: Sphagnums Capillifolium and Palustre, Philonotis Fontana, Polytrichum Commune.

Lichens: Ochrolechia Frigida, Ochrolechia Tartarea, Thamnolia Vermicularis, Cladonia Rangiferina (Reindeer Moss), Flavocetraria Nivalis.

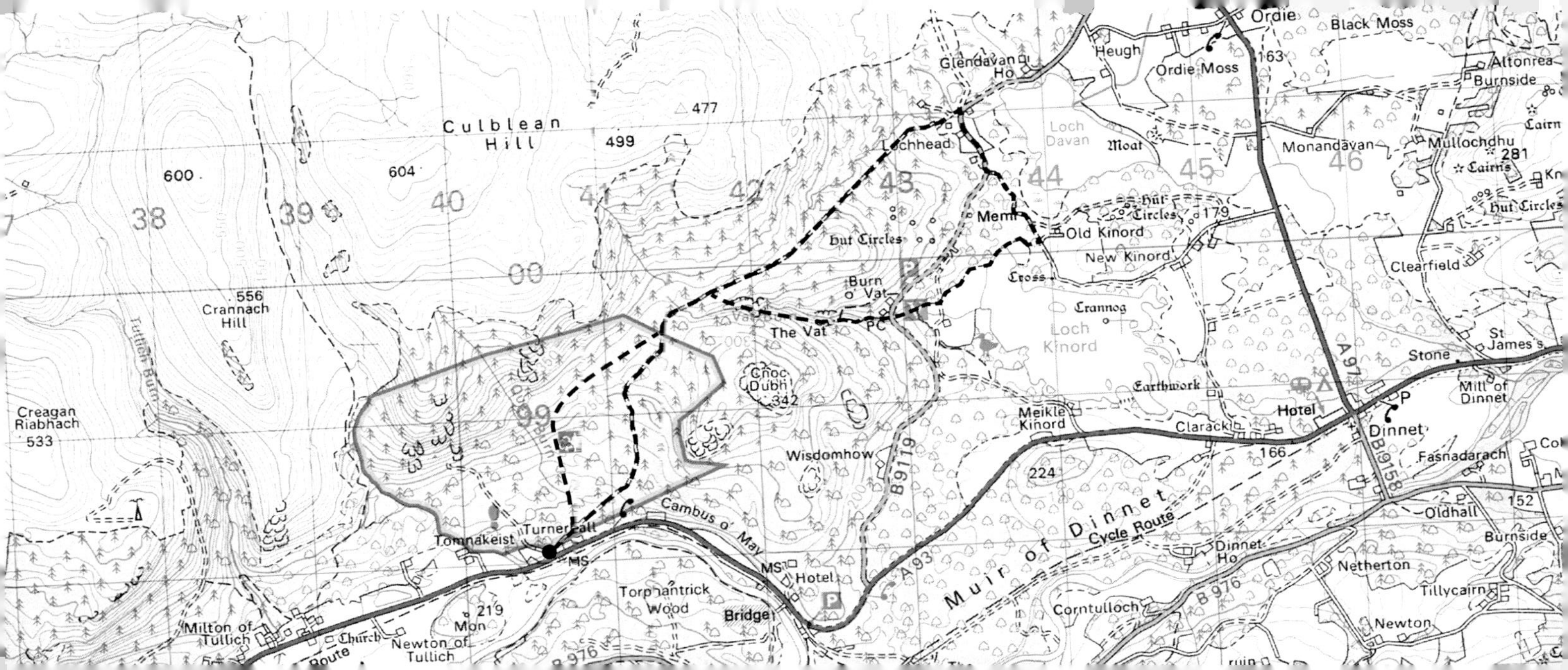
Ordie
Black Moss
Heugh
Ordie Moss
163
Altonrea
Burnside
Glendavan Ho
Loch Davan
Moat
Monandavan
Mullochdhu
281
Cairns
Cairn
Hut Circles
Culblean Hill
477
499
600
604
Lochhead
Memi
Old Kinord
New Kinord
179
Clearfield
Hut Circles
Burn o' Vat
Cross
Crannog
Loch Kinord
The Vat
PC
556
Crannach Hill
Tullich Burn
Creagan Riabhach
533
Cnoc Dubh
342
Earthwork
Stone
St James's
A 97
Mill of Dinnet
Dinnet
Hotel
Meikle Kinord
Clarack
166
Fasnadarach
B 9158
Wisdomhow
B 9119
224
Oldhall
152
Burnside
Turner Hall
Tomnakeist
MS
Cambus o' May
Muir of Dinnet
Cycle Route
Dinnet Ho
Netherton
Tillycairn
A 93
Hotel
Torphantrick Wood
219
Mon
Bridge
Corntulloch
B 976
Newton
Milton of Tullich
Church
Route
Newton of Tullich

20. MORVEN (MORBHEINN) (THE BIG HILL) LANDRANGER MAP 37

Morven is a hill which occupies a prominent position in Lower Deeside and gives good views of the Howe of Cromar and the hills to the south. (Map, Compass and Boots are essential).

9 km 3 hrs net ht 660 m

Access: Turn off at the sign marked Groddie which is 5½ km from Dinnet. Just before the road to Groddie Farm there is a large area where cars can be parked (no charge), and is the starting point for the walk (Grid Ref 410 044).

Route: Start at the gate to a large grassed area and follow the track to a ruined house called Balhennie and continue around the hill along the Coinlach Burn. The path now turns northwards and goes through to the north shoulder of the hill where the route to the summit is marked by cairns. The summit at Morven does provide adequate shelter to enjoy a break when it is cold and windy.

The return is made by the same route. As an alternative, the walk could be extended by walking down to the drove road which goes across the southern slopes of Morven from Lary to Bridgefoot which is a short distance from Groddie. The drovers would have descended to the Tillypronie and then taken a road now destroyed which would have taken them to Groddie then to Bridgefoot. From there they would have gone over the shoulder of Morven and then on to Lary and Glen Muick or Glen Shee.

Geology: Unlike other hills in the area, Morven is composed of norite, a "basic" rock containing iron and magnesium. Lower down on the eastern face of the hill there is a strata of diorite, a rock which also contains magnesium. It is the presence of these rocks together with other calcareous rocks that ensures that Morven is covered in grass. It is a Site of Special Scientific Interest because a large area of the hill is covered by juniper, a shrub which grows in calcareous soil.

Flowers: Heather, Cloudberry, Bearberry, Blaeberry (Bilberry), Dwarf Cornel, Stone Crop, Cranberry (Cowberry), Chickweed Wintergreen, Devil's-bit Scabious, Heath Bedstraw, Cross-leaved Heath, Lousewort, Starry and Yellow Saxifrage, Rosebay Willowherb, Heath Spotted Orchid, Hare's Tail Cotton Grass.

Club Mosses: Fir 1,300m, Alpine 1,200m, Stags Horn 840m, Interrupted 1,000m, maximum height of growth.

Mosses: Sphagnums Capillifolium and Palustre, Philonotis Fontana, Polytrichum Commune.

Lichens: Ochrolechia Frigida, Ochrolechia Tartarea, Thamnolia Vermicularis, Cladonia Rangiferina (Reindeer Moss), Flavocetraria Nivalis.

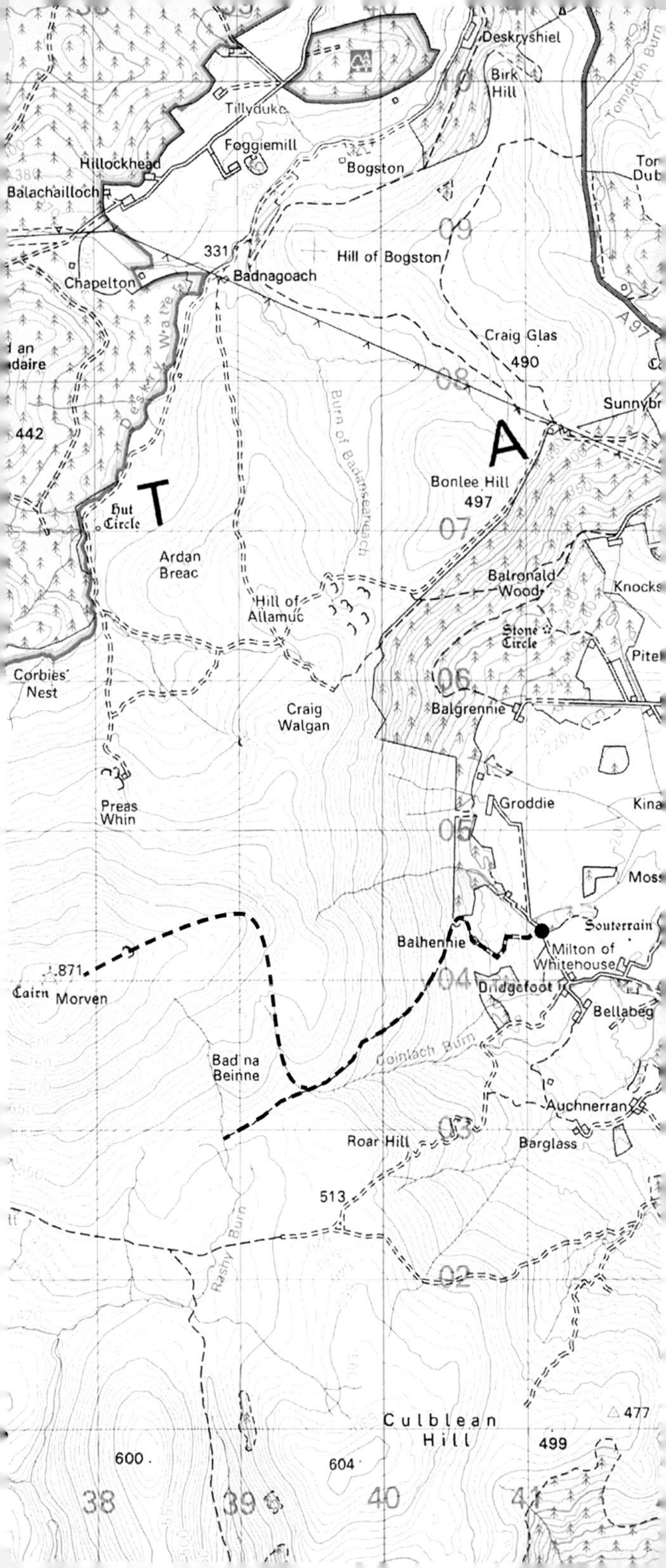

Deskryshiel
Birk Hill
Tillyduke
Foggiemill
Bogston
Hillockhead
Balachailloch
Hill of Bogston
331
Badnagoach
Chapelton
Craig Glas
490
Sunnybr
Tor Dub
A97
Burn of Badanseannach
A
Bonlee Hill
497
442
T
Hut Circle
Ardan Breac
Balronald Wood
Knocks
Hill of Allamuc
Stone Circle
Pite
Corbies' Nest
Craig Walgan
Balgrennie
Preas Whin
Groddie
Kina
Moss
Souterrain
Balhennie
Milton of Whitehouse
871
Cairn Morven
Bridgefoot
Bellabeg
Coinlach Burn
Bad na Beinne
Auchnerran
Roar Hill
Barglass
513
Rashy Burn
Culblean Hill
477
499
600
604
38
39
40
41
10
09
08
07
06
05
04
03
02

21. TILLYPRONIE TO BADNAGOACH LANDRANGER MAP 43

The walk to Badnagoach has been included as it was an important resting place for drovers coming from the north and then going to over the shoulder of Morven to Lary and then to mounth roads which led to cattle markets in the south. It is a short walk which starts at Tillypronie and goes over the shoulder of Bonlee Hill, descends to Badnagoach then goes over the Hill of Allamuc and then descends to Tillypronie.

12 km 3 hrs net ht 200 m

Access: Take the A93 which goes from Dinnet to Glenbuchat and turn into the woods on the Morven side at the signpost to Migvie. This is a good track which has space for parking and which is the starting point for the walk (Grid Ref 422 073). Return to the A97 and walk up for a short distance, where there is a track going through the trees and up the hill. This levels out at the top of the hill and enters moorland. This badly eroded track was used by the drovers and had been well maintained at one time. It descends into Glen Deskry and joins another track at a point opposite Badnagoach Farm. Turn left up this track and go around the Hill of Allamuc. The track now turns eastwards to where it meets a track beside a dyke on the other side of which is a plantation. Go along the path at the side of the dyke to where it rejoins the old drove road which came from Badnagoach and now goes to the parking area.

Geology: In Glen Deskry the underlying rock is olivine and gabbro which are calcareous rocks. From Badnagoach to the Hill of Allamuc and down to Tillypronie. The underlying rock is norite, a rock containing iron and magnesium which provides nutrients for the grass on Morven.

Flowers: Heather, Cloudberry, Bearberry, Blaeberry (Bilberry), Dwarf Cornel, Stone Crop, Cranberry (Cowberry), Chickweed Wintergreen, Devil's-bit Scabious, Heath Bedstraw, Cross-leaved Heath, Lousewort, Starry and Yellow Saxifrage, Rosebay Willowherb, Heath Spotted Orchid, Hare's Tail Cotton Grass.

Club Mosses: Fir 1,300m, Alpine 1,200m, Stags Horn 840m, Interrupted 1,000m, maximum height of growth.

Mosses: Sphagnums Capillifolium and Palustre, Philonotis Fontana, Polytrichum Commune.

Lichens: Ochrolechia Frigida, Ochrolechia Tartarea, Thamnolia Vermicularis, Cladonia Rangiferina (Reindeer Moss), Flavocetraria Nivalis.

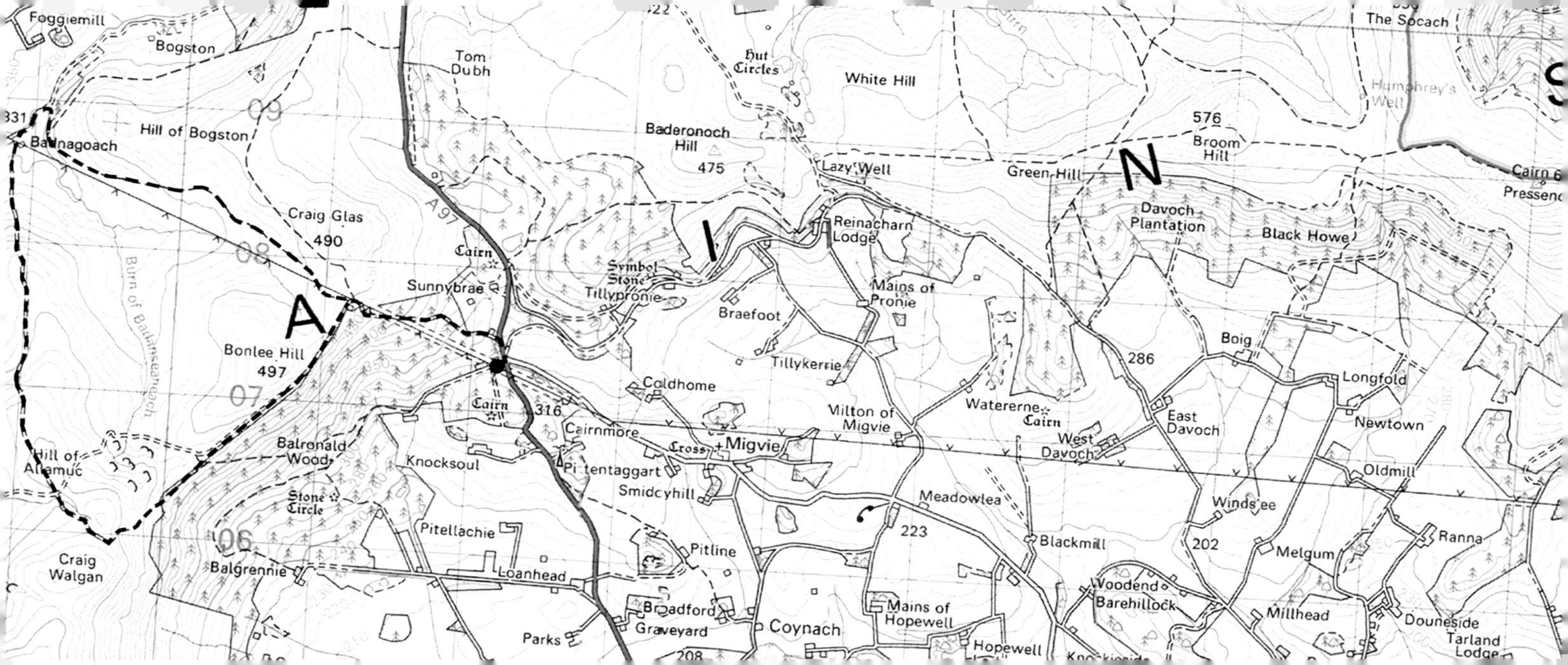
Foggiemill
Bogston
Hill of Bogston
Balnagoach
331
09
Tom Dubh
Hut Circles
White Hill
The Socach
Humphrey's Well
576
Broom Hill
Baderonoch Hill
475
Lazy Well
Green Hill
N
Cairn
Pressend
Craig Glas
490
08
A97
Cairn
Symbol Stone
Tillypronie
Sunnybrae
I
Reinacharn Lodge
Davoch Plantation
Black Howe
Mains of Pronie
Braefoot
Tillykerrie
A
Bonlee Hill
497
07
Burn of Badanseanach
Cairn
316
Coldhome
Milton of Migvie
Watererne Cairn
286
Boig
Longfold
Newtown
East Davoch
West Davoch
Cairnmore
Cross
Migvie
Balronald Wood
Hill of Allamuc
Knocksoul
Pittentaggart
Smidcyhill
Meadowlea
Oldmill
Winds'ee
Stone Circle
Pitellachie
223
Blackmill
202
Melgum
Ranna
06
Craig Walgan
Balgrennie
Loanhead
Pitline
Woodend
Barehillock
Broadford
Graveyard
Parks
Mains of Hopewell
Coynach
Millhead
Douneside
Tarland Lodge
Hopewell
208

APPENDIX 1

FORMATION OF THE LANDSCAPE OF UPPER DEESIDE

The story of Upper Deeside and the wider Cairngorms area began over 700 million years ago when mud and sands were deposited in a vast ocean. These were buried by more mud and sand, and compressed into rocks, known as 'Dalradian' rocks. Then, between 460 and 425 million years ago, the ocean disappeared as movements of the plates that make up the Earth's surface caused ancient continents to collide. The collisions crumpled and folded the Dalradian rocks, pushing them up to form part of a huge mountain range known as the Caledonian Mountains. They also compressed and heated the rock, altering it to become hard 'metamorphic' rock. These metamorphic Dalradian rocks are the oldest rocks in Upper Deeside.

Additionally, molten rock was produced and pushed or 'intruded' into the Dalradian rock. Some may have erupted as volcanoes, but many cooled and solidified while still deeply buried in the Earth, forming numerous 'igneous intrusions'. Over many millions of years, weathering and erosion have worn away the ancient mountains and laid bare the metamorphic Dalradian rocks and igneous intrusions which were once deeply buried. There is a particularly large number of intrusions along the Dee valley especially in Upper Deeside from the huge granite mass which underlies much of the Cairngorm Massif, to the granites underlying Lochnagar, Glen Gairn and Ballater. Magnesium and iron-rich 'basic' intrusions are thought to occur due to an ancient fault line along the Dee valley channelling the rising molten rock.

The heat from the molten intrusions produced very hot water, rich in dissolved minerals, which circulated through cracks in the cooling and solidifying intrusion. Within the Cairngorm granite, these fluids are thought to have altered the granite rock around the cracks, by a process known as 'hydrothermal alteration' to form a much softer and more crumbly rock. Once the granite was exposed, these weaker, hydrothermally altered zones eroded more rapidly, forming valleys which were excavated still further by the Ice Age glaciers. Gleann Einich, the Lairig Ghru, Glen Avon, Glen Derry and Lairig an Laoigh are all thought to follow the lines of hydrothermal alteration zones later affected by erosion.

As the igneous intrusions were cooling, the large continent of which Scotland formed a tiny part, was moving from south of the equator, northwards. Scotland passed through sub-tropical and tropical climates to its current, more northerly, position.

As the continent drifted north, the Caledonian Mountains were eroded away by wind and water to form a landscape of low relief near to sea level. Around 65 million years ago, the continents of North America and Europe began to separate, and the North Atlantic Ocean first appeared. An unusual hot upwelling of material from deep in the Earth at the same time caused Scotland to be 'jacked-up' and tilted to the east while many volcanoes erupted along the west coast. Upper Deeside and the wider Cairngorms area were raised up to form a high gently undulating plateau at the current mountain altitude. This was also a time of strong global warming which provided ideal conditions for deep chemical weathering of the bedrock. The hydrothermally altered zones in the granite masses were weathered to form wide shallow valleys in this plateau surface.

Around 23 million years ago the climate began to cool and 2.6 million years ago the Ice Age began. During cold periods of the Ice Age much, or all, of Scotland had a permanent snow cover and powerful glaciers filled the glens. However, there were also warm periods *(see diagram)* when the climate and snow cover would have been much as they are today. The movement of the glaciers and the water produced when the ice melted in warmer periods, shaped much of the landscape we see today. The most severe erosion was caused by glaciers, which cut today's deep glens into the gently rolling plateau surface, sometimes straightened them to leave 'truncated spurs' such as Devil's Point. In contrast, relatively little erosion occurred on the summit plateaux. This is particularly true in the eastern part of the Cairngorms area where granite tors are still found, for example on Ben Avon and Lochnagar. These were formed either before the Ice Age or during its warmer phases, but were not flattened by glacial erosion.

Corries formed during periods of less extensive ice cover, in north and east facing slopes where snow accumulated and lay longest. Freeze-thaw action broke the granite of the high plateaux into jagged 'block fields', as can be seen on Derry Cairngorm. It also moved loose material down-slope forming distinctive sheets, terraces and lobes found, for example, in many places on Lochnagar. Water from melting ice cut channels and gorges. Some of these, such as Clais Fhearnaig and Poll Bhat are now left high and dry, while others, such as the rock gorges at Linn of Dee and Linn of Quoich, are still being excavated, though much more slowly, by present-day rivers. Blocks of ice left buried in debris by retreating glaciers eventually melted leaving deep depressions known as 'kettle holes'. These now often form small lochs such as Loch Phadruig.

The last major cold period of the Ice Age, when a large ice sheet covered all of Scotland, peaked around 22,000 years ago, with all the ice having melted again by 14,000 years ago. However, a brief cold snap followed between 12,900 and 11,500 years ago during which small glaciers formed in the high mountain corries of the Upper Deeside and wider Cairngorms area. After the last glaciers melted, unstable slopes, exposed when the ice melted, collapsed in massive rock falls leaving large boulders jumbled into piles, for example in the Lairig Ghru and at Loch Etchachan. Plants began to re-colonise the area, gradually forming deeper, more productive soils. Grasses and sedges were followed by dwarf shrubs and then birch, hazel and finally pine woodlands.

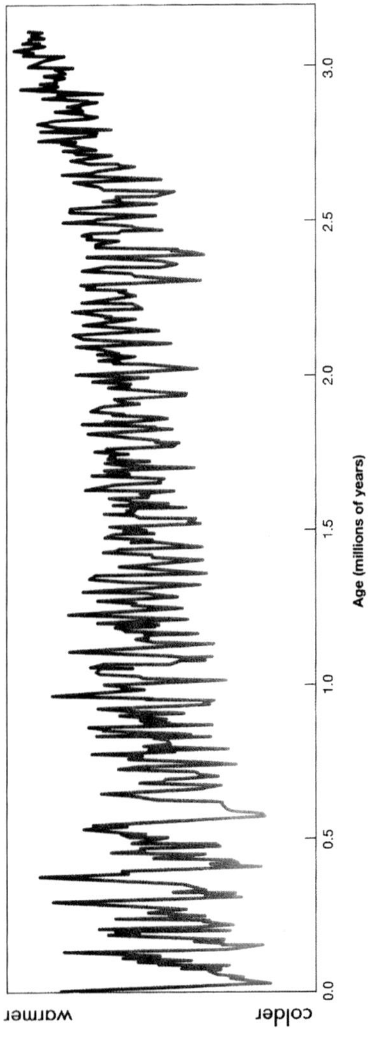

Climate change during the Ice Age interpreted from a sediment core from the floor of the North Atlantic. The climate has switched regularly between colder and warmer conditions.

APPENDIX 2

SHIELINGS

The transfer of livestock to higher ground in the late spring so that they can feed on fresh grass has been carried out in Scotland as far back as the 12th Century. This practice has been long-established in Scandinavia and the Alpine areas of Europe, and is still carried out in Austria. With the introduction of improved methods of farming which provided grazing for cattle, this practice died quite early in the South of Scotland. It continued in the North due to the short and unreliable growing season and the uncertainty of getting sufficient revenue to pay the rent and obtain food. Farmers in the 17th and 18th Centuries depended upon the sale of their cattle for which there was a continuing demand.

Cattle, sheep and goats were sent to the shielings in May, where the grass was fresh which enabled the cattle and the sheep to provide a crop of calves and lambs which were to be fattened and brought back in July to be sold in the markets in Crieff and Falkirk. The other reason why the livestock were sent away, was that their departure allowed the ground to be ploughed and the seed sown for crops of oats, bere (an early form of barley), and pease (which also provided nitrogen for the soil).

Women and children accompanied the livestock to the dwelling sites which had already been prepared by the men. There was plenty of work to be done, cows had to be milked and cheese made which was used to pay the rent. This was taken back by the men who came regularly to bring food such as oatmeal and turnips. The children ensured that the livestock kept to their allotted areas. Firewood and lichens were gathered to provide dyes for the cloth which would be woven in the winter, as well as young heather to make ropes which were always needed in a farm.

The dwellings in Glen Connie appear to conform to others in the area. Each was approximately 25 feet long and ten feet wide, although there were some larger buildings in some areas of Glen Dee. There was usually also a small building (8 x 6 feet) beside the dwelling or part of it, to store the butter and cheese. There would have been a resident cat to keep down the mess. The base of the house was made of a double row of stones about 15-18 inches wide and about 18 inches high. The back wall was banked up by grass covered earth and inside the floor was hollowed out. In every case, the site was on high ground and situated beside a burn. The wall of the dwelling would have been built up using stones from the burn and the hillside, and turf to make it windproof. For the roof, they would have taken up each year, curved timbers called "cruicks" the end of which would have rested on the walls. The structure would then be covered with heather to bind all the branches together to form a roof and then it would have been clad with turf. The result was a warm and waterproof dwelling. One half of the floor was devoted to living and cooking. A layer of heather provided a comfortable base in the sleeping area.

There are many shieling sites in Glen Ey, Glen Connie, Glen Lui, and the Baddoch. Apart from the latter, where Invercauld Estate records show some 64 sites, there is apparently no evidence to show how the sites were allocated to the tenants of farm touns and larger units. The Royal Commission for Ancient and Historical Monuments in Scotland (RCAHM) map of shieling sites on Mar Lodge and Invercauld Estate show many groups of sites, and it may be that the tenants of settlements with more than one tenant, built the dwelling beside one another and their livestock shared a common area of grazing. The map shows two main groups Allt Cristie Mor and Allt Connie. These sites still retain the grass areas that acted as paths between the shielings. There are however many scattered sites in the area and the occupants may have kept a small area of grass beside the site which is now overgrown by the heather.

Note: The Royal Commission for Ancient and Historic Monuments in Scotland has a web site given below, which shows the location of items of archaeological interest in each Scottish parish.
www.rcahms.gov.uk-pastmap

APPENDIX 3

LIME KILNS

Settlements in Upper Deeside during the 17th and 18th Centuries had a low yield from their crops which was barely sufficient to feed their families and livestock. The reasons were that there were too many settlements, each with too small an area of land, a short growing season, cool, wet summers and a lack of winter feed such as hay and turnips. Farmers therefore devoted their time to rearing the small, black cattle for which there was a ready market and the income enabled them to pay the rent and buy food.

By the middle of the 18th Century land owners were increasingly not renewing the leases of tenants, but they were giving tenancies for larger farms on condition that the land was enclosed, drained and lime applied and crops rotated. The transition from the runrig system to enclosed farms markedly reduced the number of people working on the land and many tenants were dispossessed.

Sources of limestone were available in Upper Deeside which had to be extracted from rig ground and transferred to a kiln, together with the necessary fuel, such as peat which provided the best fuel or whatever was at hand, e.g. birch. Fir was for the Laird. Means of transportation were limited in the early days and roads did not exist which could have taken carts so the only method of transporting the stone and fuel was by manual labour.

In the early days, the type of kiln used was called a "clasp", a round structure about eight foot in diameter and constructed of rubble, e.g. stones taken from fields. It was constructed by making a depression in a piece of ground and laying a double ring of stones around it and filling the area with brushwood. A space was left for an air intake and a further layer of stones would be added and a layer of peat. The limestone which had been broken down into small pieces would then be laid on top of the peat.

The "clasp" or clump kiln was inefficient as the rubble walls allowed the heat to escape so that the limestone, depending upon its position, would be subjected to varying degrees of heat, resulting in some of the limestone remaining unconverted. When the fuel was burnt, the kiln was demolished and the limestone allowed to cool. This process reduced the weight of limestone by half. It then had to be broken down, a process that produced a lot of dust, which caused damage to the eyes, skin, throat and nose. In the latter part of the 19th Century, "Draw kilns" were used which were much larger structures set into banks, where possible, to reduce heat loss. They had a large draw hole at the front which served as an entrance to fill the kiln and also to control the intake of air.

It was not until the latter part of the 18th Century that commercial kilns were built and an adequate road system introduced. With the advent of the railways and the availability of lime from agricultural merchants in Aberdeen, the use of kilns declined sharply.

APPENDIX 4

PLANTS

Plants: The list of flowers given with each walk represents only a small number which are likely to be seen and it is advisable to carry a flower guide as an aid to identification. The 15 photographs were chosen as detailed descriptions of them are given in "Hostile Habitats" *(see Recommended Reading).* Flowering times have not been given as they vary according to factors such as altitude and weather.

Club Mosses: The plants look like large mosses but unlike them, have root systems and take nutrients through veins. The 'club' is part of the shoot where its spores are produced so they are more like ferns than mosses.

Mosses: Mosses are small soft plants that are typically 1-10 cm tall, although some species are much larger. They usually grow close together in clumps or mats in damp or shady places. They do not have flowers or seeds. A few species are wholly aquatic and others like sphagnum inhabit bogs and marshes and are much larger than other mosses, reaching 8-10 inches.

Lichens: Lichens are different from other plants and mosses because they are actually made up of a fungus and an alga living and growing closely together (known as symbiosis). If you grow the fungus or the alga separately in the laboratory they look nothing like the lichen. The characteristic shapes, forms and colours develop only when they are together. The fungal partner forms most of the lichen body (called a thallus) while the algae usually grow in a discrete layer close to the surface of the thallus. In the lichen symbiosis both partners benefit from being together; the alga gains protection from the environment by living with the fungus while in return it supplies the food products of photosynthesis to the fungus.

Many walkers will be familiar with the Club Mosses, Mosses and Lichens which are seen particularly on all the walks, although unable to identify more than a few. As there are a very large number of these plants, it was decided to list only a few representative ones and provide their photographs. As many other varieties will be seen, walkers are advised therefore to take photographs of those which are interesting and search the following websites for more information.

Club Mosses: British Pteri Doccical Society

Mosses: www.britishbryologicalsociety.org.uk

Lichens: British Lichen Society – http://www.thebls.org.uk

Definitions of Geological Terms

Calcareous Rock: Rock containing calcium carbonate as well as other minerals.

Dolomitic Limestone: A rock containing calcium carbonate and magnesium which has metamorphisised.

Metamorphism: The process which changes a rock as a result of pressure and/or heat.

Pluton: large mass of molten rock.

Schist: Rock which originally contained a lot of clay which, when metamorphisised contains a large amount of flakes of mica.

APPENDIX 5

BIRDS

Names Supplied by Courtesy of the Royal Society for the Protection of Birds, Aberdeen.

Walks 1 & 2: Common Sandpiper, Curlew, Dunlin, Green Woodpecker, Meadow Pipit, Oystercatcher, Ptarmigan, Rock Pipit, Ring Ousel, Snipe, Wheatear.

Walk 3: Buzzard, Common Sandpiper, Curlew, Dunlin, Golden Eagle, Golden Plover, Kestrel, Meadow Pipit, Ptarmigan, Ring Ousel, Wheatear, Rock Pipit.

Walk 4: Dotterel, Common Sandpiper, Golden Plover, Golden Eagle, Meadow Pipit, Ptarmigan, Red Grouse, Ring Ousel, Wheatear.

Walk 5: Buzzard, Chaffinch, Common Sandpiper, Curlew, Golden Eagle, Goldcrest, Golden Plover, Kestrel, Lapwing, Meadow Pipit, Rock Pipit, Ring Ousel.

Walk 6: Buzzard, Common Sandpiper, Dipper, Goldcrest, Golden Plover, Ring Ousel, Meadow Pipit, Red Grouse, Stonechat, Spotted Flycatcher, Sparrowhawk, Wheatear.

Walk 7: Buzzard, Chaffinch, Dipper, Golden Eagle, Green Wagtail, Golden Plover, Kestrel, Ring Ousel, Stonechat, Sparrowhawk, Black Grouse, Goldcrest.

Walk 8: Buzzard, Chaffinch, Dipper, Curlew, Goldcrest, Golden Plover, Meadow Pipit, Ring Ousel, Stonechat, Snipe, Twite, Wheatear, Wigeon.

Walk 9: Buzzard, Black Grouse, Coal Tit, Curlew, Golden Eagle, Greenfinch, Spotted Woodpecker, Redstart, Stonechat, Ring Ousel, Spotted Flycatcher, Pied Wagtail.

Walk 10: Black Grouse, Buzzard, Curlew, Golden Eagle, Ring Ousel, Kestrel, Lapwing, Redshank, Redstart, Stonechat, Treecreeper, Wheatear, Wigeon.

Walk 11: Black Grouse, Chaffinch, Common Sandpiper, Coal Tit, Goosander, Green Wagtail, Meadow Pipit, Pied Wagtail, Stonechat, Wheatear, Sparrowhawk, Siskin.

Walk 12: Black Grouse, Coal Tit, Goldcrest, Golden Eagle, Golden Plover, Spotted Woodpecker, Kestrel, Meadow Pipit, Redstart, Stonechat, Siskin, Wigeon.

Walk 13: Buzzard, Coal Tit, Goldcrest, Golden Eagle, Golden Plover, Spotted Woodpecker, Kestrel, Meadow Pipit, Redstart, Stonechat, Siskin, Wigeon.

Walk 14: Buzzard, Curlew, Goldcrest, Golden Plover, Kestrel, Jay, Long-tailed Tit, Meadow Pipit, Wigeon, Wheatear, Red Grouse, Stonechat.

Walks 15/16: Buzzard, Chaffinch, Coal Tit, Jay, Long-tailed Tit, Goldcrest, Great Tit, Meadow Tit, Meadow Pipit, Stonechat, Treecreeper, Great Spotted Woodpecker, Kestrel.

Walk 17: Golden Eagle, Goldcrest, Kestrel, Hen Harrier, Jay, Long-tailed Tit, Meadow Pipit, Pied Wagtail, Redstart, Ring Ousel, Stonechat, Treecreeper.

Walk 18: Ring Ousel, Buzzard, Dunlin, Goldcrest, Golden Eagle, Hen Harrier, Jay, Long-tailed Tit, Lapwing, Merlin, Ring Ousel, Redstart, Wheatear.

Walk 19: Buzzard, Coal Tit, Curlew, Goldcrest, Golden Plover, Jay, Long-tailed Tit, Ring Ousel, Red Grouse, Stonechat, Tawny Owl, Wigeon.

Walk 20: Buzzard, Hen Harrier, Kestrel, Curlew, Dunlin, Golden Eagle, Golden Plover, Ptarmigan, Ring Ousel, Stonechat, Merlin.

Walk 21: Buzzard, Curlew, Great Spotted Woodpecker, Oystercatcher, Sparrowhawk, Dunlin, Goldcrest, Great Tit, Lapwing, Coal Tit, Siskin, Kestrel.

Polytrichum Commune

Sphag Palustre

Ochrolechia Tartarea

Philonotis Fontana

Sphag Capillifolium

Flavocetraria Nivalis

Alpine Clubmoss

Fir Clubmoss

Ochrolechia Frigida

Stag's-horn Clubmoss

Interrupted Clubmoss

Cladonia Rangiferina (Rein Moss)

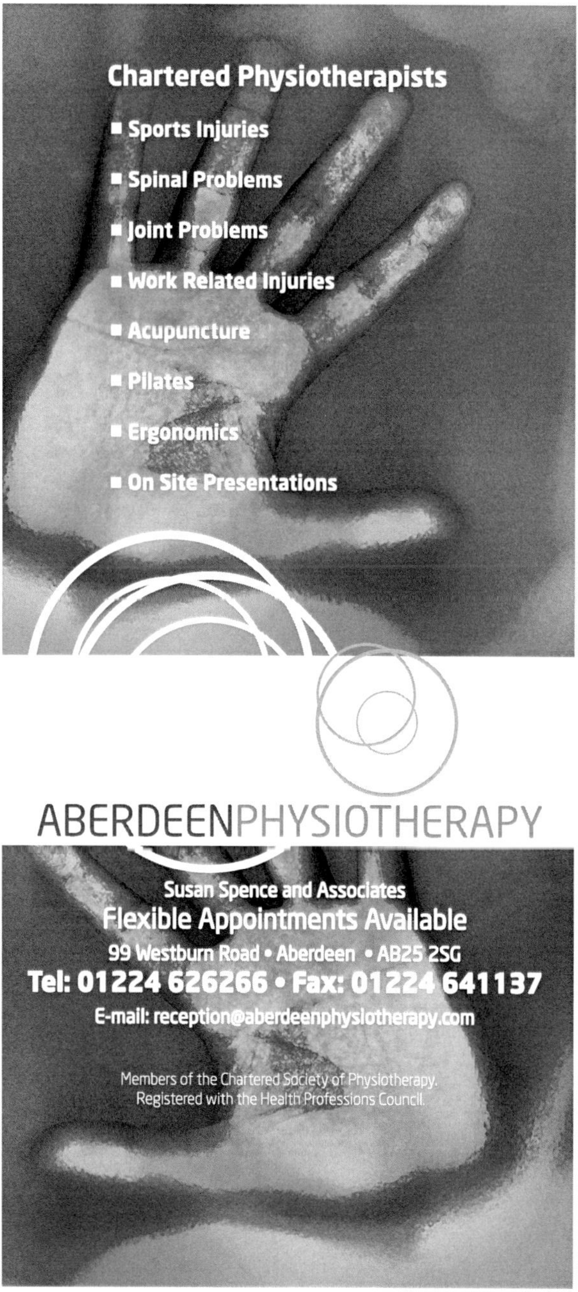
Chartered Physiotherapists
■ Sports Injuries
■ Spinal Problems
■ Joint Problems
■ Work Related Injuries
■ Acupuncture
■ Pilates
■ Ergonomics
■ On Site Presentations
ABERDEENPHYSIOTHERAPY
Susan Spence and Associates
Flexible Appointments Available
99 Westburn Road • Aberdeen • AB25 2SG
Tel: 01224 626266 • Fax: 01224 641137
E-mail: reception@aberdeenphysiotherapy.com
Members of the Chartered Society of Physiotherapy.
Registered with the Health Professions Council.

KELLY OF CULTS

In 1902, Benjamin Kelly founded his family business based on the principles of Quality, Value and Service.
At Kelly of Cults, some things never change.

- Award-winning Supermarket and Bakery at:
  345, North Deeside Road, Cults, Aberdeen, AB15 9SX
  Tel.: 0845 456 1902 (lo-call rate) Fax: (01224) 869864
  ALL YOUR GROCERY NEEDS PLUS BAKERY, BUTCHERY, WINE & SPIRIT AND FRUIT & VEG. DEPARTMENTS
- Bakery Shop and Tearoom at:
  257, North Deeside Road, Peterculter, AB14 0UL
  Tel.: (01224) 733100
  FRESH BAKERY AND EXCELLENT COFFEE TO SIT IN OR TAKE AWAY
- Petals of Peterculter Flower Shop at:
  299, North Deeside Road, Peterculter, AB14 0UL
  Tel. & Fax: (01224) 733222
  FLOWERS FOR ALL OCCASIONS FROM OUR QUALIFIED, PROFESSIONAL FLORISTS
- Cults Post Office at:
  324, North Deeside Road, Cults, Aberdeen, AB15 9SE
  Tel. & Fax: (01224) 867110
  ALL YOUR POST OFFICE NEEDS PLUS EURO AND US DOLLAR CURRENCIES OVER THE COUNTER, CREDIT CARDS, PHONE SERVICES, INSURANCE, PASSPORT CHECKING AND MORE

POTARCH

HOTEL & RESTAURANT

Coffee | Lunch | Dinner
Real Ale | Malts | Beer Garden
Log Fire | Rooms

Walkers & Ramblers Most Welcome!

Open 7 Days
10.30am to 11pm

By Banchory, AB31 4BD

01339 884339

www.potarchhotel.co.uk

NOTES

NOTES